Eric Chappell's

RISING DAMP

A Celebration

Dedicated to the memory of
Leonard Rossiter and Richard Beckinsale

Eric Chappell's

RISING DAMP
A Celebration

by
RICHARD WEBBER

First published 2001 by Boxtree
an imprint of Pan Macmillan Ltd
Pan Macmillan, 20 New Wharf Road, London N1 9RR
Basingstoke and Oxford
Associated companies throughout the world
www.panmacmillan.com

Published in association with Granada Media Commercial Ventures

Rising Damp is a Yorkshire Television Production

ISBN 0 7522 6139 8

3 5 7 9 8 6 4 2

A CIP catalogue record for this book
is available from the British Library.

Designed and typeset by seagulls
Printed and bound in Great Britain by MacKays of Chatham plc

CONTENTS

ACKNOWLEDGEMENTS

First and foremost I would like to thank Eric Chappell for letting me write a book about his brilliant sitcom. Eric has been generous with his time and support of this project, and without his help this book wouldn't have got off the ground.

As well as my agent, Jeffrey Simmons, and everyone at Boxtree, especially Katy Carrington, I would like to thank all the actors, relatives of deceased actors and members of the production team who gave up time to talk about their experiences of *Rising Damp* – in particular, Ronnie Baxter, Vernon Lawrence, Len Lurcuck, Ian MacNaughton, Colin Pigott, Brenda Fox, Peter Hardman, Olive Simpson, Colin Philpott, Don Clayton, Quentin Newark, Rod Saul, Terry Knowles and Linda Crozier.

Other people who've helped and deserve thanks include John Duncan, Una Wilson, David Scase, David Wanless and Issy Berry at Yorkshire Television, Stephen MacDonald, Roy Skeggs, Joe McGrath, Roger Symons, John Tydeman, Caroline Cardis, Paul Sample, Rupert Hitzig, Alan King and Peter Stone. And special thanks to Ian Abraham, whose knowledge and exhaustive research for his own magazine and the official *Rising Damp* website has proved valuable – and I enjoyed all the chats, too.

Finally, I am very grateful to Sir Paul Fox for writing the Preface and to Charlie Catchpole for agreeing to write the Foreword. Thanks to both of you.

RICHARD WEBBER

PREFACE

When I arrived at Yorkshire Television as the new Director of Programmes, the comedy department – such as it was – was bereft of ideas and programmes. I sent for my old BBC friend Duncan Wood. He was Head of Comedy there, having pioneered such wonderful programmes as *Hancock's Half-Hour* and *Steptoe and Son*, programmes that will be classics for ever. I persuaded Duncan to join me at Yorkshire Television and at once I was hopeful.

In a drawer in his desk at Leeds, Duncan found the script of a show called *The Banana Box*, written by Eric Chappell. This became *Rising Damp*, thanks to some wonderful scripts by Eric, the brilliant casting of Leonard Rossiter, Richard Beckinsale, Frances de la Tour and Don Warrington, plus the role of Duncan Wood as executive producer.

The first series was not quite the success we had hoped, but, in an unusual move for ITV, we persevered and at once commissioned a second series. This time, in a better slot in the schedule, the show took off.

Ronnie Baxter produced the first three series and then Duncan, in his wisdom, changed producers and brought in Vernon Lawrence, another old friend from the BBC, who produced the final series, by which time *Rising Damp* was a major success. We were the envy of our colleagues in ITV. There was a tussle about where the show should be played: during the week, when Thames, Granada and Central were the principal companies, or at the weekend, when LWT was keen to have the show. Yorkshire had never been in such a position before.

I am delighted this book tells the story of *Rising Damp* and pays tribute to two great actors who, sadly, are no longer with us: Leonard Rossiter and Richard Beckinsale. Fortunately, thanks to Channel 4, *Rising Damp* is being shown again, for the fifth occasion at peak time. I cannot think of another show which remains required viewing more than a quarter of a century after it was launched.

SIR PAUL FOX, CBE

FOREWORD

What makes a classic sitcom? How to explain that magical chemistry by which an idea, a script and a cast somehow fuse together to produce a programme which captures the public's imagination, and lives on for years, even decades, in our memories? A show which, like *Rising Damp*, possesses such enduring qualities that it can be repeated apparently endlessly and yet still seem as fresh and funny as it did the day it was first screened.

Of course, a brilliantly conceived situation, a superb writer (or writers) and first-rate actors are a help. But none is necessarily a guarantee of success.

Some long-forgotten (and best-forgotten) flops were penned by top writers. Who remembers *Lance at Large*, a vehicle for Lance Percival, which was an early collaboration by the great David Nobbs (*The Fall and Rise of Reginald Perrin, A Bit of a Do*) and Peter Tinniswood (*I Didn't Know You Cared*)? Or *Our Kid*, written by the brilliant *Billy Liar* team of Keith Waterhouse and Willis Hall?

Good actors who have been miscast can sabotage the finest scripts. Felicity Kendal is arguably the nation's best-loved sitcom actress. Leslie Phillips is a master of his craft. Writer Michael Aitkens penned the poignant, bitter-sweet *Waiting for God*. Yet when they combined to offer us *Honey for Tea*, the result was a turkey of Bernard Matthews proportions.

As happens too often in sitcom land, the situation here was so unlikely – Kendal as a rich American putting her thick son through an Oxbridge college, where Phillips was the preposterous Master – that audiences simply could not believe a word of it. Eric Chappell's genius in *Rising Damp* – honed on his stage play *The Banana Box*, which spawned the series – was to pick a situation that was all too believable: an anonymous, squalid house divided into seedy bedsits, owned by a penny-pinching, sneering, socially inept and insecure landlord, who bullied and cheated his male tenants and lusted hopelessly after the lone female.

The characters were real. Rigsby, the obnoxious creep, was as loathsome, mean-spirited and pathetic as those other great monsters of the

Britcom, Alf Garnett and old man Steptoe. Everyone knew a cocky, none-too-bright charmer like Alan, or a prim, pursed-lipped, unworldly maiden-aunt figure like Miss Jones.

Philip, the mature student, was a master-stroke. Suave, dapper, patently more intelligent, better educated and socially superior to his tormentor Rigsby – and black. Rigsby's loathing and fear of Philip was compounded by his tenant's claim to be the son of an African chief, stirring up nightmarish thoughts of savagery and the jungle in Rigsby's fevered little brain.

Let's bear in mind how brave this was in the early seventies, when black faces were rarely seen on British TV, except in menial or stereotypical roles. In our own politically correct age, I very much doubt whether a modern-day Rigsby would be allowed to voice his contempt and disgust towards a member of an ethnic minority. Yet, back then, nobody complained. Because the joke was always on Rigsby. Philip continually got the better of him, thus reinforcing his superiority and Rigsby's inadequacy.

So it was with Rigsby's lecherous intentions towards Miss Jones. The predator always ended up the loser, slinking away with his tail between his legs.

Many sitcoms from the seventies, shown again today, date horribly. The humour of *The Liver Birds,* for instance, seems as alien to me now as the ridiculous hairstyles, flares and kipper ties. Yet *Rising Damp* continues to work its magic more than a quarter of a century later, not only because the jokes are so good and the acting flawless, but also because the quartet of characters are simply timeless, with their recognizably human desires, aspirations and failings striking a chord with every generation.

Richard Webber's labour of love deserves a place on the bookshelf of everyone who appreciates the art of making great television. His research has been breathtaking, detailing not just every bit-part player who passed through every one of the twenty-eight episodes, but listing the too-often unsung technicians, the cameramen and lighting operators, who all contributed to the show's success.

As Rigsby himself would say, 'My – y – y God!'

CHARLIE CATCHPOLE,
TV critic for the *Daily Express*

INTRODUCTION

After tirelessly entertaining viewers for nearly thirty years, one could excuse Eric Chappell's classic sitcom *Rising Damp* for showing signs of age. But, just like other members of that small band of vintage comedies which march relentlessly through the decades providing endless laughs, Rigsby and Co. remain full of vitality. The show's accessibility and freshness continue to attract new admirers, paving the way for regular repeats on mainstream and satellite TV, the release of videos, audio cassettes and this book, the first to be published about the making of the show. Such success delights Eric. 'Who would have thought in those cold, draughty seventies we would see in the new millennium with *Rising Damp* still on TV?' he said to me during a recent interview. He has every right to be proud of his creation, because each time you watch an episode it seems to get better.

When you consider why certain shows endure the passing of time unscathed while less fortunate examples drop over the precipice into obscurity, the reasons are usually the same: in addition to top-notch scripts, solid ensemble acting and a plot based largely on reality and not on a situation so fantastic that an audience can't understand or appreciate it, every successful sitcom must contain sufficient degrees of conflict from which humour can stem. Eric's scripts explored a range of issues from race, class, education and depression to prosperity, sex and age. Most of these issues were evinced through Rigsby, the seedy landlord whom Eric once described as a 'lonely, pathetic figure'. A middle-aged man whose life has been peppered with disappointments and regrets, Rupert Rigsby envies the freedom enjoyed by his younger lodgers, creating a heightened conflict because they're living under the same roof. Always claiming he was trying to run a 'respectable house', Rigsby was one of life's biggest bigots, brimming with petty hates and jealousies. If he was missing out on life's pleasures, he was determined to spoil his tenants' hopes by banning members of the opposite sex in rooms for starters.

In this central character, Eric created one of TV's most memorable individuals. The landlord from hell was always snooping around,

INTRODUCTION

poking his nose into his tenants' affairs. Constantly barging unannounced into their rooms (none contained locks, not even the bathroom, which meant tenants had to sing while taking a bath) he was forever playing the overbearing father-figure to his overgrown children,
dishing out unwanted advice and views. As with many comedic cre-
ations, including Steptoe and Alf Garnett, the public formed a love–
hate relationship with the character. Although most people rejected
Rigsby's narrow-mindedness and unjust manner, his few redeeming features carried him through, with audiences feeling sorry for him when
his plans turned sour.

There is no doubt that an episode of *Rising Damp* affords the viewer
real value for money. Each of the twenty-eight instalments bulge at the
edges, packed with rich, fast-paced dialogue; the episodes fly by and
before you know it the closing credits begin to roll, leaving the viewer
longing for more. The speed and energy within the show were generated by the script and actors, most notably Leonard Rossiter, the kernel
of the sitcom's success. His rate of delivery was such that Eric had to pen
extra pages of script because he devoured the dialogue at rapid speed.

If Rossiter was the driving force behind the show, his fellow performers were equally adept in their portrayals of tenants unfortunate
enough to find their lives being played out in Rigsby's Dickensian
boarding house. With a main cast boasting just four characters, the
sitcom couldn't afford any weak links. From Eric's strength of characterization and the actors' fine performances, a close-knit group of individuals with a strong dynamic quickly established themselves. Casting
obviously has a fundamental bearing on a programme's future and, just
like other shows that can rightfully be termed classic, *Rising Damp* got
the mix just right. The inordinate skills of Rossiter were beautifully complemented by the other three team members. Rigsby may have been a
loud, domineering character, but he was forever being tripped up by
those cleverer and subtler than him.

Rossiter was unbeatable in his role. His highly developed skill at
physical comedy, the subtlety of his facial expression and his impecca-
ble timing combined with his assiduous performance week in, week out
to reveal a character who was lonely and vulnerable, traits also found in
his heart's desire: Ruth Jones. Low in self-confidence, Miss Jones clung
to the distant dream that one day she'd find her knight in shining
armour, and De la Tour played the character beautifully.

Richard Beckinsale's performance as Alan was a perfect counterpoint to Rossiter's. Quiet, assured and relaxed, he provided the ideal antidote to Rigsby's manic qualities. Don Warrington's performance became increasingly assured and polished as the sitcom progressed, an admirable achievement bearing in mind he wasn't long out of drama school.

With all the scenes being acted out within the confines of the poky boarding house, it's indicative of the acting and standard of scriptwriting that you never tire of *Rising Damp*. Only great thespians make the art of acting appear effortless, but they can't do it without a supply of top-quality scripts. Even when the heat was on and Eric was writing two sitcoms simultaneously, he never resorted to churning out potboilers. As a result, *Rising Damp* has established itself as one of the timeless classics of British sitcom.

RICHARD WEBBER, June 2001

1

ERIC CHAPPELL – THE WRITER

Eric Chappell's storytelling skills were honed in the playground through necessity. 'I started telling stories at school as a way of avoiding being bullied,' he says. 'The school I attended in Grantham was tough and if you weren't popular for something people tended to pick on you. I was quick with my tongue so kept out of trouble by being entertaining.'

Born in the Lincolnshire town of Grantham in 1933, Eric grew up in an environment not particularly conducive to budding writers. 'I come from a working-class background and my mother didn't really approve of writing; she thought it unwise to put something on paper in case it was held against you at a later date,' explains Eric. 'Being a discreet lady, my wanting to write worried her a bit.'

However lacking the household was in terms of literature, Eric had a happy and caring upbringing and adopted his father's enthusiasm for sport. 'Dad was sports-mad and that's where he got his drama from – he didn't need books.' It was Eric's teacher back in the 1940s who helped him explore and develop his interest in story writing. 'We had to stand up in class and tell stories, and the first time I did it I spoke for an hour – I couldn't stop; all these words just poured out of me. I based my story on all the different books I'd borrowed from the library, although I added some ideas of my own. All the other kids enjoyed my stories so much I was asked to do it on a weekly basis.'

As the school years passed and Eric moved on to secondary education, other interests took priority. 'Sport took over as time went on,' he admits, 'and we did little serious English at secondary school, so any thought of writing took a back seat for a while.' It wasn't until Eric had left school and started working for the East Midlands Electricity Board that he returned to his stories. 'I was in my mid-twenties and studying accountancy, which was pretty soul-destroying. I wasn't a good book-keeper. I was fine with the essays on law and economics, things like that, but struggled with my maths and accountancy. I got very depressed and failed my finals, so I thought, "Sod this! I'll do what I want to do with my life."'

For years while working as an auditor for the electricity board, Eric was secretly forging his future via his typewriter, telling no one that he was trying to become a writer. During the day he worked in the audit department, travelling around branches from Leicester to Coventry. After checking the cash and stock he compiled a report for head office, before returning home to try his hand at penning novels. 'They were bad novels and, looking back, I'm ashamed of them; they weren't good enough for publication.'

After receiving yet another rejection slip in 1969, Eric decided it was time to change course. 'Novels take so much writing, it's demoralizing when they're rejected. I just couldn't face another two years trying to write a book; I didn't seem to have the energy any more.' Eric remembers the time he was lying in the bath, thoroughly depressed, when the thought of trying something new came to him. 'I suddenly said to myself: "Why don't I write a play. For one thing, it's only 20,000 words instead of 70,000."'

Within a short period his first play was completed; now he had to decide what to do with it. After reading the biography of R.C. Sherriff, Eric decided to send the play to Curtis Brown, a London literary agency. 'Sherriff went to Curtis Brown with his first play and they sounded a decent bunch of blokes, so I thought I'd give them a try,' he explains.

It was read by John Bassett, who surprised Eric with his response. 'He must have seen something which no one else ever saw, because he liked it. I must admit, I didn't think it was any good at all.' Eric was shocked when he was invited along to Bassett's London office to discuss the play. 'I nearly had a heart attack!' he says jokingly. 'My heart raced as I entered his office, but I was pleased because John's enthusiasm and assurances were the first time anyone had told me I could write.' Although Eric felt he lacked the narrative gift needed for novel-writing, he started believing he had the ability to succeed as a play-wright. 'I wasn't very good at describing people through words, but what I could do was echo what people said to each other, making it sound real, from which a scene could be created. I think the secret in life is to find something you can do well and then give it all you've got; it's no good trying to do anything else because you'll always end up in second place. It's a difficult choice because sometimes the things you do badly seem more attractive.'

Titled *A Long Felt Want*, the work focused on two young boys and their growing awareness of girls, but the play was never produced, a fact that doesn't surprise its author. 'It was very much a beginner's piece of work. I hadn't written any comedy or dialogue like that before, and it showed.' The play never got off the ground, but Eric took consolation from the reaction it caused among those who read it. 'They didn't get that bored look that was evident whenever they read one of my novels: there was an air of what I can only describe as respect.'

Even though *A Long Felt Want* sank without trace, Eric became a client of Bassett. 'Being able to say: "I've got an agent" made me feel so smug.' Eric started concentrating on writing half-hour plays, one of which was produced by the BBC, before he turned to a more extensive piece, *The Banana Box*, which became the precursor to the highly successful sitcom *Rising Damp*.

The play first received a rehearsed reading at the Hampstead Theatre Club, London, in November 1970, before being staged at Leicester's Phoenix Theatre the following summer. It was performed at a further five venues, finishing off with a month at the Apollo in London, by which time Leonard Rossiter, Frances de la Tour and Don Warrington were installed. Until the play opened, Eric had kept his writing ambitions secret. 'I never told a soul,' he laughs. 'In those days events happened in strange ways. I was very secretive about my writing because I was an auditor and didn't want anyone to think I was arty. If I told people I wrote plays, the response would be: "Oh, when does he find time for that?"'

There was another reason Eric kept his writing ambitions close to his chest. 'I was supposed to be studying for exams. Every so often my boss would ask whether I was studying hard and when my finals were coming up, so I led a secret life.' Only his wife knew what he got up to at weekends and early mornings, even though he knew there would come a time when all would have to be revealed. That day came when the play was being staged at Leicester and started being advertised on hoardings in the area. 'I was in Leicester talking to my boss when this bus went by; on the side it said: "*The Banana Box* by Eric Chappell". I was so embarrassed I sort of turned him away from it. I realized then that I had to tell him.'

The opportunity arose when the theatre distributed promotional leaflets advertising the play. 'I showed one to my boss, who glanced at it for a while, then looked up and said: "It's the same name as yours, Eric." I told him it was me, and he replied: "Oh." He was the sort of person who wouldn't say any more than that.' Gradually news got out that Eric was a writer. 'One by one people edged up to me and asked whether I'd written a play.'

One of his workmates lived four doors down the road, and when he got home he told his wife there was a playwright living in the road. 'The funny thing was that when asked to guess who it was, she thought it was my wife.'

With the prospect of having his first stage play enter the West End, and the arrival of a few minor commissions in the form of radio plays, Eric left the electricity board in 1973. 'I had some money from the pension scheme and worked out that I could survive for two years. My wife got a job with Oxfam – which I thought was particularly apt, with starvation being on the horizon! – and things started looking OK. Perhaps if I'd been better paid at the electricity board I wouldn't have had the nerve to leave. I left and worked out I had enough in the bank to pay me a salary for two years, but my wife having a job meant I could survive almost for ever. I gave myself two years and if I hadn't made it by then I'd return to auditing.'

Giving up a steady job didn't meet with universal approval. His work colleagues thought Eric 'mad'. 'Everybody felt I was crazy except my wife!' he admits. 'She wanted me to do it, while my parents reminded me that I had two kids and couldn't simply give up my job.' People he knew at work treated his decision as an act of escapism. 'I'm not an escapist, and wasn't out to change my life because I couldn't stand it. I'd been planning this for years but wasn't going to take such a big step until I knew I had enough skill as a writer.'

For the first two years of his new career as a full-time writer Eric worked at the dining-room table. But as the years passed he decided he needed somewhere more conducive to producing successful scripts. 'I got myself an office eventually, but found myself returning to the kind

4

of environment I thought I'd left behind at the electricity board. But I needed an office because working in the dining room back at home became too distracting.'

Eric, who admits to being a pessimist, must have thought twice about whether he'd made the right decision to quit his auditing job when the first play he wrote for television was rejected. 'It was a love story for ATV and when it was turned down I thought: "My God, is this what it's going to be like? I write a play and it gets sent back and I don't get the money."' Knowing he had to learn from this experience, he spent the weekend rewriting it and sent it back to ATV. 'Luckily, they accepted it. I've never had a nervous breakdown in my life, but if it had gone on like that, who knows,' Eric said with a smile.

The early 1970s saw Eric turn his attention from stage plays to television comedy, and by 1974 he was writing two sitcoms: *The Squirrels* (set in the accounts department of a television hire company and focusing on office politics, this won him the Pye TV Award for Most Promising New Writer) for ATV and *Rising Damp* (which won the BAFTA Award for Best Situation Comedy) for Yorkshire Television. But his first piece of television comedy was *The Spanish Dancers*, a one-off play for HTV, starring Henry McGee, who later played Seymour in *Rising Damp*. 'I'll always have a soft spot for Bristol, where the programme was recorded,' says Eric. 'It was a funny half-hour play. I sent it to my agent, who liked it, and he sold it to Harlech.' The play wasn't networked, but it was a sign that Eric's career was starting to happen, albeit slowly.

Although he knew the financial rewards were more lucrative in television than theatre, and writing for the small screen seemed the logical career step, the pressures of writing to tight schedules worried Eric at first. It wasn't a decision he took lightly. 'Writing plays at that point didn't seem to carry the same pressure: I'd complete the script for myself and then submit it to my agent. But once I was working on the two sitcoms for television it became all about due dates: you sign the contract, get a portion of your money, you agree to deliver by a certain date and suddenly you're on a treadmill. At that point in my career I had two contracts, two delivery dates, an even bigger treadmill.'

Working to a commission brought security, but pressures reminiscent of his previous career. 'There were all these dates and promises to meet and fulfil and it was suddenly like working for the electricity board again, only worse.' The heat was on and every minute of the day was spent writing scripts. 'I never went out of the house; I didn't even go shopping on a Saturday morning because I had to get on. Not only did I have to write the scripts, I was desperately thinking up ideas for the next.'

Launching your television sitcom career with one show is enough for most people to cope with, but Eric, now with a new agent, Bryan Drew, had both pilot scripts picked up, although *Rising Damp* took more of his time. 'Shaun O'Riordan, who directed *The Squirrels*, accepted the scripts as they stood, whereas *Rising Damp* took more time to get right, which probably explains its success. I liked *The Squirrels*, but doing two shows was one too many, so I dropped it after a couple of years.'

After the success of *Rising Damp*, Eric felt driven to prove he had another hit series in him. He showed that when *Only When I Laugh* pulled in greater audiences than *Rising Damp*. Twenty-nine episodes of the hospital sitcom were transmitted by Yorkshire, beginning in October 1979. Starring James Bolam, Peter Bowles, Christopher Strauli and Richard Wilson, the show was based on Eric's memories of staying in hospital as a boy and visiting wards thereafter. 'Figgis [played by Bolam] was very similar to Rigsby in many ways, someone who'd seen it all, and it was closer to *Rising Damp* than perhaps I realized.'

Just like its predecessor, *Only When I Laugh* began as a play. 'I always write the play first – or try to, because sometimes they aren't completed – because it imposes all sorts of disciplines on you which are good when it comes to writing the sitcom.'

The style of Eric's writing and his economical use of sets and situations characteristically lend themselves to the stage. Even if one of his programmes hadn't originated from the theatre, it could have been adapted for the medium. But for his next project, he continued in his usual fashion and wrote a play first. *We're Strangers Here* was a critical success when it was screened by ATV, and Eric persuaded Vernon Lawrence, who'd directed the final series of *Rising Damp*, *Only When I Laugh* and Eric's two-series sitcom *The Bounder*, written for Peter Bowles, to commission a series, titled *Duty Free*. Twenty-one episodes, spread over three series, and a Christmas Special, were transmitted of this holiday sitcom between 1984 and 1986. It reached number one by the fifth show and was nominated for a BAFTA. '*Duty Free* was always enormously popular, and if it had been made by the BBC, it would have been repeated for ever,' says Eric.

Eric has seen many of his sitcoms work successfully abroad. An American version of *Home to Roost*, starring Jack Klugman, was produced for NBC in 1986–7 and ran to twenty episodes on the US Network. A German version of *Only When I Laugh* was produced in 1993, a Swedish version comprising twenty-four episodes has been recorded, and a Norwegian version has also been created. Elsewhere in Europe, Dutch television has transmitted its own versions of *Only When I Laugh, Duty Free, Home to Roost* and *Singles*, while Portuguese productions of *Rising Damp* and *Singles* have been warmly received.

Nowadays Eric travels each day to his nearby office, where he concentrates on writing stage plays. Recent productions include *Up and Running* and *Haunted* starring Keith Barron, *Something's Burning* with Joanna Van Gyseghem, *Natural Causes* and *Theft* with George Cole.

Eric still lives in his native Lincolnshire, and during a busy career has written over two hundred comedy scripts and more than a dozen stage plays – and he's still writing.

TELEVISION WORKS

The Spanish Dancers (half-hour play for HTV, transmitted in 1971)

Rising Damp (Yorkshire TV, 1974–8, twenty-eight episodes)

The Squirrels (ATV, 1974–7, fourteen episodes)

Only When I Laugh (Yorkshire TV, 1979–82, twenty-nine episodes)

Misfits (Yorkshire TV, 1981, seven episodes)

The Bounder (Yorkshire TV, 1982–3, fourteen episodes)

We're Strangers Here (ATV play)

Duty Free (written with Jean Warr; Yorkshire TV,
1984–6, twenty-two episodes)

Natural Causes (Yorkshire TV play, 1988)

Home to Roost (Yorkshire TV, 1985–90, twenty-nine episodes)

Singles (written with Jean Warr; Yorkshire TV – except pilot by
Thames, 1984 – 1988–91, twenty-two episodes)

Haggard (Yorkshire TV, 1990–2, fourteen episodes)

Fiddlers Three (Yorkshire TV, 1991, fourteen episodes)

STAGE WORKS

The Banana Box (1971)

We're Strangers Here (1976)

Natural Causes (1984)

Up and Running (1988)

Something's Burning (1992)

Haunted (1994)

Theft (1995)

It Can Damage Your Health (1995)

Heatstroke (1995)

Haywire (1997)

Double Vision (2000)

2

THE BANANA BOX

Venues
Hampstead Theatre Club, London
(a rehearsed reading on Sunday 29 November 1970)
Phoenix Theatre, Leicester (25 May–12 June 1971)
Adeline Genée Theatre, East Grinstead (12–19 March 1973)
Oxford Playhouse, Oxford (20–31 March 1973)
Theatre Royal, Newcastle (9–16 April 1973)
Hampstead Theatre Club, London
(17 May–16 June 1973. Preview 16 May)
Apollo Theatre, London (25 June–24 July 1973)

Cast
Hampstead Theatre Club, London (rehearsed reading):
Rooksby.....................Peter Woodthorpe
Noel...........................Geoffrey Burridge
Philip.........................Clifton Jones
Ruth ....Heather Canning
Lucy...........................Nina Baden-Semper
Directed by John Tydeman

Phoenix Theatre, Leicester:
Rooksby.....................Wilfrid Brambell
Noel Parker ....Keith Drinkel
Philip Smith..............Neville Aurelius
Ruth Jones ....Janet Michael
Lucy...........................Louise Nelson
Directed by Stephen MacDonald

**Adeline Genée Theatre, East Grinstead,
Oxford Playhouse and Theatre Royal, Newcastle:**

Rooksby......................Leonard Rossiter
Noel Parker ....Paul Jones
Philip Smith..............Don Warrington
Ruth Jones ....Rosemary Leach
Lucy...........................Elizabeth Adare
Directed by David Scase

Hampstead Theatre Club and Apollo Theatre, London:

Rooksby......................Leonard Rossiter
Noel Parker ....Paul Jones
Philip Smith..............Don Warrington
Ruth Jones ....Frances de la Tour
Lucy...........................Elizabeth Adare
Directed by David Scase

Overview (as presented in the script)

The Banana Box is a play for three men and two women. When Noel
Parker, a young student, arrives to take up residence in the digs he
had visited earlier he is somewhat disillusioned, both with the rooms
and with the landlord, Rooksby. His disillusionment increases when
he finds he is to share; and finally he discovers his partner is a young
black man, Philip. A working relationship, however, develops
between them. Philip, reputedly the son of a Chief, is an object of
interest to Rooksby, who enjoys picturing wild ideas of his life and
tribal habits. There are also two girls: Ruth (white) and Lucy (black)
who have their part in his life. Finally it transpires that Philip's chief-
tain is a myth, and he himself comes from no further away than
Croydon. Noel and Lucy go off together and even Ruth deserts him.
But there is Rooksby, still eager to indulge in his imagining of exotic
behaviour in Philip's 'country'.

2: THE BANANA BOX

Eric Chappell was still working as an auditor for the electricity board when he struck upon an idea for a play. It was a hot summer's day in 1969 and he'd just finished a job in Leamington Spa when he stopped for a bite to eat. While tucking into a sandwich he glanced at the local rag and an article caught his eye. 'It was a story about a black guy who had stayed as a hotel guest for twelve months by posing as an African prince. He'd been received with a great deal of fuss and respect; it was a great story and I thought it could be developed into a comedy.'

He recalls reading a political book around the time he was searching for an appropriate title for the play. The derivation of the title dates back many years to a time when prejudices were rife, as he explains: 'It was based on objections "Little Englanders" made towards the influx of the Irish in the 1920s and 1930s. The argument even extended to people who had been born in England. The remark that was made to counter this was: "If a cat has kittens in a banana box, what do you get: kittens or bananas?" In other words, these people were arguing that being born here didn't make you English.' He found this an interesting observation, and plumped for *The Banana Box*.

Eric envisaged writing a play along the lines of the Victorian farce *Charley's Aunt*, but with a full-time job to hold down, he didn't pursue the venture for several months. When he eventually put pen to paper in 1970, the play took on a completely different complexion to the story he'd read in the newspaper. 'Instead of basing the story in a posh hotel, it became a seedy lodging house, which was more my style!' The landlord's make-up, meanwhile, was an amalgam of Eric's own thoughts and the characteristics of someone he knew. 'He didn't become a fussy, blazered hotelier but a rather seedy, old sweat. He was influenced by someone I knew and with whom I could identify.' Eric admits that the real-life character wasn't as invidious or wretched as Rigsby became. 'When I started working just after the war some people still had contempt for all things foreign, so I experienced some eye-opening stories and observations. I took all this old-sweat cynicism and gave it to Rooksby.'

The success of Eric's sitcom has made the name Rigsby synonymous with the unkempt side of 'bedsitland', but the character started life as Rooksby. 'It's an unusual name and sounded slightly Shakespearian; I knew one or two people called it and it seemed ideal for one of my characters.'

The Banana Box was Eric's first stab at a full-length stage play and he found it a challenge. 'It wasn't easy and took longer than antici-pated, partly because I was working during the day for the electricity board. It was about three months before I'd completed it, which might not sound long, but is when you've already got a full-time career.' Too tired in the evenings, Eric worked every weekend and got up at six each morning to write before heading off to work; research, meanwhile, was conducted in the local library. 'I didn't know any African or black people, so I borrowed books on African customs, took interesting little stories and gave them to Philip in the play. There was a ring of authen-ticity about the whole affair, although in the play he was bogus, an ele-ment we never really explored in the television series. Philip wasn't really an African prince: he was just an ordinary guy, probably West Indian, who decided to glamorize his past, just in the way that Rooksby did. That was the whole point of the play: they were both posing; while Rooksby was posing as a war hero, which he obviously wasn't, Philip was pretending to be an African prince. They were both outsiders, really, Philip because he was black in a white society, and Rooksby because nobody liked him.'

Initially Eric intended that no one character become the lead, but inevitably the sheer strength and vividness of Rooksby saw him assume this mantle. 'I was going to make it even-handed. Philip was, in many ways, the interesting character – he was the mystery guy.'

The Banana Box came early in Eric's writing career, at a time when he was still getting to grips with characterization, plot and dialogue. It was his first stage play and inevitably posed constant challenges, none more so than having to create his first female character, Miss Jones. 'Never having written a female character before, I didn't know how to deal with Miss Jones at first. So I made her coy and fastidious just as a counterpoint to Rooksby.'

If the play was to see the light of day on stage a theatrical produc-tion company was required to finance it. Eric's agent, John Bassett, endeavoured to interest a suitable party, including the highly respected producer Michael Codron. The play was placed in the shop window on Sunday 29 November 1970, when it was given its inaugural performance at the Hampstead Theatre Club, at the Swiss Cottage Centre, London. As the curtain lifted at 6.30pm, the audience sitting in their six-shilling seats watched the birth of what was to become one of the country's greatest sitcoms, with the one-page programme setting the scene with the simple sentence: 'Student rooms in a lodging house in a university town. The present.'

Given the role of directing this rehearsed reading was former BBC producer John Tydeman, who had produced Eric's first radio play, *Like Achilles*. 'I knew John Bassett and Michael Codron, who was interested in the play, so was asked to direct it.' Tydeman feels the play was a success. 'I did the casting and was able to come up with some very good people: Peter Woodthorpe was very popular, Clifton Jones was probably the best-known black actor at the time, while Heather Canning was well known at the National Theatre.'

Even though Tydeman didn't envisage *The Banana Box* being adapted into a television series, he admired the script. 'It was a terrific success and I think we had a full house. It was funny and unusual for its time and the style of humour a little more upmarket than what you see in *Rising Damp;* the play was rather offbeat and worked beautifully.'

Reflecting on the play's eventual success as a television sitcom, Tydeman is not particularly surprised. 'It worked incredibly well on TV. It still possessed a demanding style of humour, and the way Eric developed the situation was clever.'

The first man to play Rooksby was character actor Peter Woodthorpe. He remembers the play partly because of the short notice he was given. 'John Tydeman contacted me a few days beforehand; initially I wasn't too sure but he persuaded me. I was very busy at that time and had little chance to prepare, so it wasn't a performance in depth, it was simply a reading.'

Rehearsed readings were all about presenting a play to the audience, usually without sets, where the actors reading from the script try to bring the characters alive. The first reading of *The Banana Box* was a success, as far as Peter was concerned. 'We got a tremendous amount of laughter, and I was gratefully relieved that I'd got through it, bearing in mind the short notice I had. But I feel I held the stage very well with it, although whether I held it to the author's pleasure, I don't know.'

The rehearsed reading achieved its goal when a London management company, headed by Michael Codron, bought the rights to stage the play. To test the water before making a commitment to bring the show into the West End, the play was staged in a regional theatre. It was offered to the Phoenix Theatre, Leicester, which snapped it up, news that excited Eric. 'I couldn't believe it when my agent told me,' he says. 'To be honest, I didn't even know who Michael Codron was at the time, which shows how green I was.'

The Banana Box was directed by Stephen MacDonald, his first play as the Phoenix Theatre's Director of Productions. Stephen had spent two years as an associate director at the theatre and looked forward to taking over the reins. In the original programme he commented: 'I am delighted that for my first production I have found a new play by a new writer' and pointed out that *The Banana Box* was the 'first "home-grown" product to have its first showing at the Phoenix'. He felt that 'quality and locality coincide' in Eric's play.

'I thought it would be interesting to find out if work originating in or around Leicester would tempt Leicester people to come and see the production, and whether it would mean anything to them,' explains Stephen, who remembers clearly the day he was offered *The Banana Box*. 'It was thrown across a room at me and landed on my desk!' he says. Robin Midgley, the departing Artistic Director, shared an office with Stephen. One bleak winter morning Midgley opened a packet that had arrived on his desk. It contained Eric's script, but knowing he had a full programme before his impending departure, he passed the script to Stephen, who recalls: 'My initial thought was that *The Banana Box* was an unlikely title; it was lunchtime when I started looking at it, not with much enthusiasm, I might add. But I started to laugh and continued reading it after lunch. Robin eventually asked what I was laughing at and I told him the script was extremely funny. I knew it was a play I wanted to direct. Here was a strong writer, and he was on my own doorstep, so I got in touch.'

Stephen met Eric, discussed the play and offered suggestions as to how, in his view, it could be improved. 'I told Eric he could write, there was no doubt about that: his jokes were good and characters interesting. However, I felt he'd written a series of good scenes, most of which worked, some didn't; but to write a two-hour play, you can't just write a series of good moments, it has to be the whole scenario. I remember saying: "As it stands, this is material for a television series, but for a play there needs to be more development of the characters' relationships and how they affect one another."'

He worked with Eric on the proposed changes, meeting regularly and helping shape the script into a format suitable for the stage. 'Eric

2: THE BANANA BOX

worked at the alterations very conscientiously while I started assembling the cast.'

Even though Stephen was excited about the play, not everyone at the Phoenix had the same enthusiasm. 'Some people felt it was too far out, too different. It wasn't a classic, like many of the other shows we'd staged, but it had its own rhythm and attitudes which were slightly surreal. It was also very funny and I just thought Eric had talent.' As soon as Stephen secured Wilfrid Brambell (alias Albert Steptoe) to play Rooksby, the opposition suddenly died.

Bringing Brambell into the frame was down to Stephen and Michael Codron, but Stephen had initially considered Leonard Rossiter, who was to join the cast later. 'He was married to Gillian Raine, with whom I had worked in my very first job; she was a fine actress, a funny lady and very good to work with and I thought she and Rossiter might be a good pairing for the show. I got as far as enquiring about Leonard, but he was booked.' Stephen continued his search and made a note of Brambell's name, just as someone from Michael Codron's office called. 'They asked if I'd considered Wilfrid and I told them I had but wasn't sure he'd come to Leicester. Thankfully he was very enthusiastic about the play.'

Keith Drinkel, Neville Aurelius, Janet Michael and Louise Nelson completed the cast. 'I'd worked with Janet at Glasgow's Citizen's Theatre; she was a good friend and I admired her work. Keith had worked for a friend of mine at Birmingham Rep. I saw him play Horatio in *Hamlet* alongside Richard Chamberlain in the lead role. Chamberlain was very good, but I thought Keith was even better. He'd just done a popular television series, *A Family At War*, for Granada and I was keen to work with him. I was planning to offer him Romeo and various other attractive parts, so I asked whether he would come early and start with *The Banana Box*, which he read and liked.

'Neville, who played Philip, was also a good actor. We're talking nearly thirty years ago, when it was unusual for a black actor to play a leading role in an English play, but he was great and we worked very happily together. He played the part well, giving the character a sort of sexual arrogance. And Louise Nelson, whom I liked, was a sympathetic Lucy.'

David Isaacs, a journalist with the *Coventry Evening Telegraph*, concurred with Stephen's views, writing: 'Keith Drinkel and Neville Aurelius are intelligent actors who find it easy to create atmosphere.' But he felt everyone's performance, including Brambell's, was 'outshone' by Janet

15

Michael. 'Miss Michael is a most talented comedienne who more than anyone else serves Mr Chappell most sweetly in squeezing every last joyful laugh from his lines.'

The play did reasonably well at Leicester, Stephen explains. 'It didn't do astonishing business, which is surprising when you think that *Steptoe and Son* was very popular at the time, but it more than covered itself; all the people who told me I shouldn't do it were made to eat their words.' He also felt there were other positive outcomes. 'As far as the Board of Directors was concerned it had been a very good move to stage the play: not only did we receive some good press reports, but we had persuaded Wilf to do a play at the theatre, arousing national interest; more actors were now interested in working at Leicester, and six months later Ian McKellen, Derek Jacobi and Leslie Sands joined us.'

The critics and journalists spotted potential in Eric's writing but high-lighted areas needing attention. Eric Shorter, writing in the *Daily Telegraph*, felt that 'Mr Chappell looks like a talent to watch'. However, the play was 'too discursive' and needed a more 'sharply felt line of development of dramatic action and though its theme of home counties-born blacks seeps through in an emotionally overwrought last act, it comes too late to give the comedy that theatrical shape which would affect us more deeply.'

Shorter also felt that the role of Lucy lacked 'conviction': 'It is not entirely Louise Nelson's fault… Mr Chappell's writing seems to panic at this point as if perplexed how to wind things up.'

A journalist writing for the *Leicester Mercury* also considered that the ending let down the rest of the piece. He believed the play explored too many issues and suggested that: 'if Mr Chappell had settled for simple comedy last night's premiere … would have been made more accept-able. It was when he plunged into dramatic depths that the effect was clouded by an untidy, unsatisfying ending.'

But for all the comments highlighting the ending, there was an over-whelming view that *The Banana Box* was a funny play from the pen of a writer with prospects. One of the best reviews came from B.A. Young in the *Financial Times*, who wrote: 'The framework of Eric Chappell's play is bedrock light comedy; what raises it above average is the veracity of the characters and the quality of the dialogue.'

Just like anyone learning a craft, Eric admits the play was far from perfect, something he realized from day one. 'First nights are always giddy affairs and often seem flattering because you've got a few friends there; it's a warm atmosphere and people are complimenting you. But first nights can be deceptive and there were lots of weaknesses in the play,' admits the writer, who feels they remained with the play, even when the cast included Rossiter, De la Tour and Warrington. 'I didn't handle the romantic side very well. When Rooksby or the other male characters were talking everything was fine, but when I brought a woman on, it didn't work. I hadn't got to grips with female characters, so whenever one of the girls came on, the play sank.'

Nevertheless, Eric hopes to revisit the script one day. 'It's too good a play to be left like it is. I ought to try getting it right one day before I pop off! I would spend time thinking about what went wrong on the night and correcting it.'

Although certain aspects of the play attracted criticism from some members of the press, there was widespread applause for Eric's debut as a playwright. Audiences enjoyed the production, and so did director Stephen MacDonald, who was surprised when Michael Codron told him he wasn't going to take it to London. 'After he'd seen the play, late in the run, I trapped him in my office. I said: "You've got Wilfrid Brambell and other actors who are good enough for you to take it into the West End." I was keen for a decision because I wanted Keith and Janet in my next season at the Phoenix if he wasn't going to take the play,' explains Stephen. Five minutes passed before Codron made his decision. 'He looked at me and said: "It's too much of a risk, I think I'll leave it."'

Stephen believes Codron, who was heavily involved in many hit shows at that point, thought the play required nursing and his busy work schedule prevented this. 'I think he felt, like me, that the piece needed careful handling and gentle nourishing; Eric, meanwhile, required looking after: persuading and cajoling rather than ordering or forcing, and perhaps Michael didn't have the time.'

Codron says: 'All those reasons were valid but also I wasn't convinced by Wilfrid Brambell's performance. Overall, I felt it was best not to pursue the play any further.'

Eric was disappointed at the time, but he admits Codron was right not to transfer the play to the West End. 'Even at that time I knew there was something wrong with it, and I wouldn't have wanted to risk my money on it.'

Eventually the play would be given its chance in the capital, thanks to the support of South African producer Leon Gluckman and Eric's new agent, Bryan Drew, who met Gluckman at a social function. Gluckman read *The Banana Box*, liked it and wanted to produce it. It was in March 1973, nearly two years since the play closed at the Phoenix, that the curtain rose again at East Grinstead's Adeline Genée Theatre, boasting an entirely new cast. At this juncture in the play's evolution, Leonard Rossiter and Don Warrington were brought in, while RADA-trained Rosemary Leach stepped into the shoes of Miss Jones, ex-Manfred Mann singer Paul Jones played student Noel Parker and Elizabeth Adare was Lucy.

As Eric, still working as an auditor, travelled to the theatre in his rusty Ford Anglia, he couldn't believe an actor of Leonard Rossiter's calibre was actually appearing in a play he'd penned. 'I admired him, he was a dynamic actor and I thought he'd eat the part alive. He may not have been a household name at that point, but he was known. I was so lucky having an actor of his quality playing the lead.'

Directing the play was David Scase. While Rossiter had already been signed up, Scase was responsible for the rest of the casting, including Frances de la Tour. 'She's a marvellous actress,' he enthuses. 'She was very experienced and accomplished when she joined. Paul Jones played his part well, and Don Warrington was perfect.'

Scase, who liked the script and didn't share Eric's concerns about the play's weaknesses, enjoyed working with Rossiter again. 'I had directed him at the Bristol Old Vic in *The Long, the Short and the Tall*, and the amount of energy he put into a role was unbelievable. He must have worked for hours on his performance.'

The play embarked on a short tour, covering two more venues, at Oxford and Newcastle, before it transferred, in June 1973, to London's theatreland. It was given a month's run at the Apollo, and the cast, by now including Frances de la Tour, did their utmost to make sure it was a success.

Journalist Jack Tinker felt that the play was a welcome arrival in the West End. 'None but the meanest soul could begrudge its good fortune. It has more assurance in its comedy, compassion and company than many of its present companions there.' But he added: 'Clever and funny as Eric Chappell is, he never seems to have resolved the fundamental problem of giving his play a focal point.'

Arriving in the capital during the middle of a heatwave wasn't the most auspicious of starts, and when the curtain fell for the last time, director David Scase was disappointed. 'It just wasn't getting good enough houses, partly because *Habeas Corpus* was running next door. It didn't catch on and as it costs plenty of money to carry a play until it matures, it was pulled, which was a great shame.'

THE PERFORMERS

PETER WOODTHORPE, the first actor to appear on stage as the bigoted landlord Rooksby, was born in York in 1931. He studied biochemistry at Cambridge for two years before leaving to appear in the original production of *Waiting for Godot*, a West End engagement which lasted forty weeks.

One of Britain's best-known character actors, he made his name in theatre while still in his twenties, winning many plaudits for leading performances in productions such as *The Caretaker* and *Poor Bitos*.

In recent years he has concentrated on films and television. On the big screen he appeared in productions including *Hysteria*, *The Charge of the Light Brigade*, *To Catch a King*, *A Christmas Carol*, *The Red Monarch*, *The Hunchback of Notre Dame* and *Merlin*.

His more recent television work includes playing Max, the pathologist, in the first two series of *Inspector Morse*, but he has appeared in many TV series, among them *Only Fools and Horses*, *Minder*, *Singles*, *Chance in a Million*, *Coronation Street* and *Three of a Kind*.

GEOFFREY BURRIDGE, who played Noel in the rehearsed reading at Hampstead Theatre Club, appeared in films and on television before his untimely death, at the age of thirty-eight, in 1987. On TV he played Clovis in the 1978 series *The Ice House*, Joe Prince in *Foxy Lady*, Dumain in a production of *Love's Labour's Lost*, Cyrus Asher in an episode of *1990* and Dorian in a 1978 episode of *Blake's 7*. His film credits included appearances in *Cymbeline*, *An American Werewolf in London* and *The Internecine Project*.

CLIFTON JONES, who played Philip at the rehearsed reading, has been seen on television shows such as *The Persuaders*, *Jason King*, *Survivors*, *Star Trek: The Next Generation*, *Space: 1999*, *The Professionals* and *Agony*. His film credits include *The V.I.P.s*, *Joanna*, *Innocent Bystanders*, *Sheena* and *China Moon*.

The first Miss Jones was played by HEATHER CANNING, who died of cancer in 1996. A busy theatre and television actress, Heather took elocution lessons on leaving school, before working in reps all around the country. Bigger theatre parts followed, but during her early career acting work was supplemented by other jobs, including a spell in the glass department at Selfridge's.

She joined the Royal Shakespeare Company in 1965 and worked on both the London and New York stage, while for the National Theatre she played Mom in *Long Time Gone*. She also toured Poland, Finland, Russia and the United States in versions of *The Merchant of Venice* and *Twelfth Night*.

During the 1960s Heather started being offered small parts on television, and as the years passed the work became more regular. She was seen in shows including *Clayhanger*, *Bergerac*, *Roads to Freedom*, *Boon*, *Casualty*, *The Darling Buds of May*, *A Village Affair*, *Jeeves and Wooster* and *Power Without Glory*, for which she won the TV Society of Australia's award for Best Supporting Actress. Heather also made the occasional film appearance in productions such as *The Hunchback of Notre Dame*, *Borderland* and *Miss Julie*.

NINA BADEN-SEMPER, who played Lucy for the rehearsed reading, became a familiar face to television viewers in the 1970s, when she played Barbie Reynolds in *Love Thy Neighbour*. During a four-year period fifty-six episodes were recorded of the sitcom, in which Barbie and her husband, Bill, live next door to one of the world's biggest bigots, Eddie Booth.

Nina's other television work includes an episode of *The Corridor People* in 1966, playing Felicity Rae Ingram in 1976's *Machine Gunner* and a Sister in a 1979 episode of *George and Mildred*. She has also been seen in a handful of films, such as *Kongi's Harvest* in 1970, *Carry On Up the Jungle*, in which she played a Nosha, and *The Love Ban*, in which she was a Skyline waitress.

WILFRID BRAMBELL needs little introduction because he will for ever be remembered for his fine portrayal of Albert Steptoe in fifty-nine episodes of BBC's classic sitcom *Steptoe and Son*. He was born in Dublin in 1912; his father worked in a brewery while his mother was an opera singer. His first performance was as a two-year-old entertaining wounded troops during the First World War.

On leaving school Wilfrid worked as a cub reporter for the *Irish Times* during the day and a part-time actor at the Abbey Theatre in the evenings. He later took the plunge and turned professional after securing a job at Dublin's Gate Theatre.

During the Second World War he toured with ENSA, and after the war appeared in numerous reps, including Bristol, Bromley and Chesterfield, before working in the West End and on Broadway.

His television work included *Life with the Lyons*, the 1950s sci-fi series *The Quatermass Experiment*, and *No Fixed Abode*, while his film credits include *The 39 Steps, The Three Lives of Thomasina, A Hard Day's Night, Where the Bullets Fly, Carry On Again Doctor* and *Holiday on the Buses*. Wilfrid died in 1985.

KEITH DRINKEL had just finished the long-running TV series *A Family at War*, when he was offered the part of Noel Parker at Leicester, a job he enjoyed. 'I liked Eric's script very much, and thought it worked well. It was funny and for its time quite bold. For me, coming from eighteen months in television, I needed something like *The Banana Box*,' says Keith, who felt the only weak point was the concluding scene. 'I thought it had a lot of potential if Eric could have got the ending right: it never reconciled and ran out of steam. Eric had a great facility for good lines, the characters were believable, but the ending didn't work, in my view.'

Keith, who wasn't offered the role of Noel when the play resurfaced two years later, was born in York in 1944 and studied English and drama at Birmingham University before working in rep. After two years of stage experience, he was offered his first television role, in *The Contenders*. Although he continued working in the theatre, TV began playing a bigger part in his career. He started being cast in classic serials, largely for BBC2, such as *How Green Was My Valley* in 1960. Other shows he has appeared in include *Tales of the Unexpected, Grange Hill, The Bill, Casualty, Love and Reason* and *Thatcher*, in which he played John Major. 'I did about eighteen years of television, including the third series of BBC's sitcom *I Didn't Know You Cared*, in 1978. Most work after that was either in radio – I worked for the BBC Radio Drama Company for over two years – or on stage.'

Keith is still busy in the theatre and is also turning his hand to directing. 'I'm doing something for a local production company I got involved with last year – it's very exciting.'

Scottish-born actress JANET MICHAEL was the second person to take on the mantle of playing Ruth Jones. Recruited by Stephen MacDonald for the Leicester production, she enjoyed working on *The Banana Box*. 'It was a very funny play,' says Janet, who felt it was funnier than the TV series that followed. 'It's difficult making a television series because you've got to keep the story moving for so long, but I liked playing Miss Jones on stage.'

The interpretation of the character for TV was very different from the way Janet played the role back in 1971. 'I played Ruth as very prim and proper, which seemed to complement Wilfrid Brambell's performance.' She regarded the Phoenix Theatre as an ideal venue for the play. 'It was just an open stage but very intimate because you were so close to the audience – a wonderful theatre to work in.'

Janet trained in Glasgow and began her professional career there at the Citizens' Theatre. Her wide theatrical experience has seen her appear in six West End productions, including *Teresa of Avila*, spend six years at the Leicester Phoenix, six years at Edinburgh's Royal Lyceum, a spell with the National Theatre Company and twenty-five years with the Perth Repertory Theatre. Her television work, meanwhile, includes appearances in *Taggart, High Road* and *Millport*.

Janet, who is also an experienced radio broadcaster, has fond memories of working alongside Wilfrid Brambell in *The Banana Box*. 'He was wonderful, such a dapper, wee man. He used to wear a diamond ring, beautiful suits, starched collar and tie and would have his hair slicked back; I couldn't believe it when I first met him because I knew him as Steptoe! He was very funny, off stage as well as on, and would tell the filthiest jokes – he just made a perfect Rooksby.'

NEVILLE AURELIUS, who played Philip at Leicester's Phoenix Theatre, came to England in 1952. After serving with the RAF for five years he joined the London Negro Theatre Workshop in 1965, while working at nights to finance his time at drama school.

He appeared on stage in numerous productions, including *Deep Are the Roots, Stand Up in the World* and *Benito Cereno*, and toured the Continent with theatre companies. On television he was seen in an episode of *Jason King, Softly Softly* and *Take Three Girls*, and he has also appeared in a handful of films. Neville, who now lives in America, is also a writer.

At Leicester Lucy was played by London-born actress LOUISE NELSON. Louise took up dancing and singing, working abroad, before studying at the Italia Conti Stage School and turning her attention to acting. After graduating she appeared in cabaret for a time.

Her TV work includes roles in *Z Cars, The Power Game, Troubleshooters* and *Thirty-Minute Theatre*. She has worked extensively on the stage.

For many people, PAUL JONES, who took the role of Noel for the London dates as well as the preceding mini-tour, is best remembered as the lead singer of the popular rock band Manfred Mann. He entered the world of pop on graduating from Oxford. After three years with the band he left and began a career as an actor, starring initially in *Privilege*, a film about a young pop singer.

He worked on the stage, winning votes from the London critics as Most Promising Actor for creating the role of Lieutenant Drake in the first year of *Conduct Unbecoming*'s West End run. He later played the part on Broadway.

Paul has combined a successful solo musical career with his work in the theatre.

What the Papers Said

The Phoenix Theatre, Leicester
'It is certainly a fresh piece of writing and has a sense of style and wit not found in every potential playwright.'

David Isaacs, *Coventry Evening Telegraph*

'The relationships are exclusive to the play, but I'm sure the characters could readily be recognised in many bed-sitter colonies.'

D.D., *Leicester Mercury*

'Mr Chappell ... obviously possesses a strong creative comic talent.'

Hinckley Times

'Chappell's humour has flashes of brightness and real originality... It should be emphasised that for a first stage play it is a noteworthy effort.'

Mike Fearn, *Leicester Chronicle*

'For all the flimsiness of the plot, it seems to me that *The Banana Box* is more intelligent than any comedy I've seen this year, and funnier than most.'

B.A. Young, *Financial Times*, 10 June 1971

ROSEMARY LEACH was the penultimate Miss Jones, playing the part at East Grinstead, Oxford and Newcastle. 'I thought the play was good, but I don't think I was quite right for the part,' she admits. 'I don't think Leonard liked me, but I probably annoyed him about something, I can't remember. The rest of us got on but I must have irritated him in some way. But he was a very talented man, and Frances, who took on the part of Miss Jones after me, was absolutely super, she really was. And I remember Paul Jones and Don Warrington with great affection.'

Born in Shropshire, Rosemary left school undecided about her future. 'I didn't know what I was going to do, whether to attend art school or become a teacher, like my parents. Then my eldest sister read an article in a magazine and there was a piece about RADA, so she suggested I tried that. So we both travelled to London for my audition and I was accepted.'

Rosemary's family helped support her through the training period. Her brother, who was serving overseas with the RAF, gave Rosemary his overseas allowance, and she commuted from her sister's house in Reading each day. For the first few terms she wondered whether she'd

What the Papers Said

Oxford Playhouse, Oxford
'It is bound to become Leonard Rossiter's play. He seems to know every frayed nerve-end, tic, grimace and warped passion welled up in the breast of the downtrodden social outcast ... his performance as Rooksby the landlord is a comic triumph.'

Don Chapman, *Oxford Mail*, 21 March 1973

Theatre Royal, Newcastle
'Every once in a while there comes a play which sets you back on your feet with quite a wallop. [*The Banana Box* is] one of those incredible pieces of playwriting that keeps you laughing from beginning to end ... it's not often that you find me rocking back in a theatre seat, sore from laughing and quite ready to face the next throwaway line – but it happened last night.'

Phil Penfold, *Newcastle Evening Chronicle*

What the Papers Said

Hampstead Theatre Club, London
'Mr Chappell has a gift for phrasing a paragraph, but the stylistic device, by the end of the second act, seems over-used. This is a strangely empty evening only rarely bashed into life by some flashing piece of outrageous behaviour by the indomitable Mr Rossiter.'

Michael Coveney, *Plays and Players*

'Nothing of any real consequence happens in *The Banana Box* ... but the dialogue and acting ensure its success as an amusing set of variations on a hackneyed theme.'

D.F.B., *The Stage and Television Today*, 24 May 1973

'Mr Eric Chappell has a nice line in throwaway, casual comic dialogue and although *The Banana Box* has little distinctive to say, it is nevertheless an amiable way of spending a few hours.'

Milton Shulman, *Evening Standard*

made the right choice, but by the time she graduated she knew she wanted to act.

Her first job was in 1955 at a weekly rep in Amersham, Buckinghamshire, as an acting ASM. After four months the theatre closed and she gave up acting and sold linens in John Lewis. But she was later encouraged to return to the stage at the Everyman Theatre in Reading, before embarking on a tour which ended up at a Butlin's holiday camp. Next she worked with Caryl Jenner in children's theatre, followed by a return to rep at Ayr, a period as acting ASM at Coventry's Belgrade Theatre and spells in Liverpool, Birmingham and Bristol.

Rosemary made her TV debut in an episode of *Armchair Theatre* in 1959. Her busy small-screen career includes countless appearances, including the role of Susan Weldon in ATV's *Power Game*, several series as Ronnie Corbett's wife in *No That's Me Over Here*, *Roads to Freedom*, *French and Saunders*, *Boon*, *Now Look Here*, *Life Begins at Forty*, *The Jewel in the Crown*, *The Charmer*, *The Winslow Boy*, *The Tomorrow People* and BBC's recent series *Berkeley Square*, playing Nanny Collins. Her favourites roles

What the Papers Said

Apollo Theatre, London
'There are plenty of funny lines and the director (David Scase) has whipped a pretty froth on top of the trifle. The weakness of Eric Chappell's play is that its amusing to-ing and fro-ing gives only a superficial view of growing up.'

John Barber, *Daily Express*

'The play has faults; but I warmly recommend it. It is funny, and well acted, and it is about *now*.'

B.A. Young, *Financial Times*

were in *Cider with Rosie, Swallows and Amazons, Roads to Freedom* and playing Mavis Hunt in *An Ungentlemanly Act*, which was recorded in the Falkland Islands. Rosemary has also made several films, including *A Room with a View, That'll Be the Day* and *SOS Titanic*, and done a lot of radio work.

(Leonard Rossiter and Frances de la Tour are featured on pages 68–78, Don Warrington on pages 80–2, and Elizabeth Adare on page 103.)

3

THE HISTORY
OF *RISING DAMP*

After tasting success with *The Banana Box* and a handful of other plays for radio and television, Eric Chappell turned his attention to the lucrative market of sitcom writing. 'I needed the money and wanted to give up the electricity board!' he says, smiling. But he admits the thought of penning a sitcom left him with mixed feelings: although it was an exciting prospect, it also left him feeling cold. 'I'd just had a play in the West End and there was talk of a film based on *The Banana Box*, which sounded exciting; what I didn't realize was that films rarely happened.' He also worried about whether he had the stamina to write a television series based on his stage play. 'All those shows, all those words and from one little play; I was taking on something I wasn't sure I could finish.'

Despite such concerns, Eric sat down and wrote not one, but two pilot scripts. As well as adapting his stage play, *The Banana Box*, he also pursued an idea he'd been cultivating in his mind for some time. *The Squirrels* explored the office politics found in the accounts department of a fictitious television rental company. It pipped *Rising Damp* to the post as Eric's first sitcom, but the latter was to prove more enduring. 'I called it *Rooksby* initially and sent it to several television companies, but it came back from all of them, including the BBC, with comments like: "There are too many jokes."'

Then Yorkshire Television's acting Head of Light Entertainment, John Duncan, who was also considering *The Squirrels*, came to watch *The Banana Box* on stage. 'Eric's agent, John Bassett, who I knew well, said he'd discovered this wonderful writer and invited me to see the play. At that time it was being produced in Newcastle, my home town. I'm always glad to return there, so I went up and saw it.' But John Duncan had mixed feelings. 'I didn't think it would make it in the West End; it was no good as a play. But it contained wonderful writing and was clearly the most brilliant blueprint for a sitcom: the characters were strong, the situation right – everything was in place. I admired what Eric had produced but thought it was being presented in the wrong form.'

When the show was over, John Duncan stayed behind and met the cast and crew. 'You don't tell people who've just come off stage that you think the play will be a flop, so I praised the writing and acting, which I meant, and wished them success in the West End; but I made jolly sure I had first option for television if the play didn't work out in London.'

Later he was fortunate enough to be given his chance. He met Eric and told him he didn't want to pursue *The Squirrels*, which was later transmitted by ATV, but wanted to transfer *The Banana Box* to TV. By this time Eric had written the script, *Rooksby*, which was aimed at television. But the rejection letters he had started receiving from other television companies considering his pilot script made him question the foundations on which it had been written. 'I started thinking that perhaps I'd flogged the black-and-white issues to death, and needed to focus on something new. Even though John Duncan had already picked up the idea, I wrote another script leaving out the black character, concentrating on the landlord and his experiences with the tenants instead.'

It was the new Head of Light Entertainment, former BBC man Duncan Wood, who convinced Eric to reinstate the character Philip, as the writer explains: 'He knew instinctively what worked with the general public, and said: "Eric, I've read your script. I like the idea but I think you should go with the black student – I like him." So I returned to the basis of the play, with the reactions and issues involved between the black student and the white student and landlord, which made life a lot easier because that's what the play was all about. From that point I found myself able to write the show.'

CASTING

John Duncan's background had been in documentaries and satirical shows, including *That Was The Week That Was*, and when he eventually commissioned Eric's pilot script back in 1974, he was heading for pastures new. 'I didn't feel entirely suited to light entertainment, so decided to move on, whereas Duncan Wood, who replaced me, was an experienced producer in that field. When he took over he inherited a show which had already been commissioned. It was a terrific start for him.' The new producer did a good job with *Rising Damp*, he feels. 'I had the satisfaction of discovering and commissioning it, but if I had produced it as well, I don't think it would have been nearly as good as it turned out, thanks largely to Duncan Wood.'

When it came to casting the pilot episode, all the stage characters except Lucy and Noel were required. Leonard Rossiter, Frances de la Tour and Don Warrington had appeared in the stage play and were secured for the small-screen version. 'There wasn't anyone better than Len,' says John Duncan, 'so there was no way we were going to replace him, and the same applies to the other two. Duncan Wood, though, would have been responsible for getting Richard Beckinsale.'

Eric was happy for Richard to play Alan Moore, a character based loosely on Noel Parker, once he was able to put a face to the name. 'I'd seen him in *The Lovers* and thought he was great, but when the producer told me he'd got Richard Beckinsale, I asked: "Who's that?" I knew the face but not the name.'

Richard was an ideal choice to play the naïve student Alan. His innocent, young look suited the character, and the rapport he established with the rest of the cast helped the show become a success. Producer Ronnie Baxter enjoyed working with Richard, classing him as a 'great foil for Leonard'. He says: 'Although he was such a young bloke, he carried a lot of experience into his performance. He was a wonderful feed and had the ability to make the lines sound as fresh as can be. It was as if he'd made them up that day, which is a great art for an actor. I used to marvel at his ability to work through three and a half days of rehearsals only to retain a freshness in his delivery for the recording: I can't praise him enough. He was very easy to work with.'

Although Eric knew Richard had plenty of fun making the show and was grateful for the opportunity to play Alan, he also realized the actor was desperate to progress beyond playing dewy-eyed characters. 'He'd been married once, was getting married again, this time to Judy Loe, and there he was playing an innocent man who'd seen nothing of life,' he says, 'whereas Don Warrington, not long out of drama school, was playing a sophisticate.'

Where Did Rigsby Live?

Rising Damp deftly encapsulates life in bedsitland. Squalid conditions in the back streets of an industrial town with its smoke-filled atmosphere, and, inside the house, peeling wallpaper and tacky furniture which should have been confined to the junk heap long ago – this is what living in a bedsit is all about for many people. Eric Chappell has also experienced life in a bedsit. 'I lived in one for two or three years, not like Rigsby's place, though. But it gave me ideas for the series. I've also heard students talking about landlords, with cutting the water off being the famous remark. All these experiences were valuable when it came to writing the show.'

The location of Rigsby's dilapidated warren of bedsits was never disclosed, and we never got to know the name of the road. But one thing discerning viewers did notice was that the house number changed between series one and two. In 'The Prowler' and 'Stand Up and Be Counted' it's 917, but by the second season it had been altered to 34. As the interiors remained just as shabby, we can only assume the Post Office embarked on a renumbering exercise. During the entire four series the only glimpses of the exterior we saw involved the roof and the front doorstep, but one thing was clear: the house hadn't seen a lick of paint for some time, and attracted life's deadbeats.

Rigsby always claimed there was nothing between the Urals and his three-storey house, where we find the attic room occupied by Philip and Alan, Miss Jones renting a first-floor room and Rigsby living on ground level. The basement and a room opposite Miss Jones's were rented out to other tenants from time to time.

From the depressing references to the surrounding area, as well as the bleak industrial landscape the eagle-eyed viewer could just about spot through the heavily soiled windows, the house could easily have been situated somewhere in the Midlands or north of England. Never announcing the actual locality, something that stemmed from *The Banana Box*, was deliberate as Eric Chappell explains. 'Everybody made up their own minds, some people referring to it as a Midlands town, others a northern town, and I'm quite sure that if it had been staged in Glasgow it would have been a Scottish town. I didn't want it localized too much, even though when the play was staged in Leicester it was referred to as a Leicester lodging house. Obviously it had to be a university town because there were students, but I just grabbed bits from everywhere.'

Wherever it was situated, the house was a dump. Rigsby kept spouting off about how he ran a respectable household, but the décor of his aged domicile did little to reinforce the standards he was always trying to attain. With worn towels in the bathroom and flypaper hanging everywhere, the house was hardly the Ritz, and it's a wonder Rigsby had the temerity to describe his rooms as being 'functional with just a hint of luxury, ideal for the professional class'.

Instead of plush surroundings in a picture-postcard setting, Alan, Philip, Ruth and any other unfortunate lodgers had to make the most of the sun setting behind the gasometer, and the wind blowing off the abattoir, in rooms furnished with relics from Rigsby's father's house.

Eric admits he didn't appreciate just how good an actor Richard was at the time. 'Richard had that look about him, he never looked old, and was brilliant as Alan. Len was full of manic energy and Richard could absorb it all; he was a very minimalist performer, extremely understated. Sometimes I looked for more action but now when I watch the episodes I realize how natural he was; it was a gift he had.' He also points out the calming effect Richard brought to the set, partly because he was used to situation comedy. 'Although he was young he was a veteran and a calming influence. He did everything in a natural way, and his reactions to situations on the set made you laugh – it was a wonderful quality.'

When the sitcom first hit the screens, journalist David Isaacs congratulated the writer and production team for the assembled cast. He wrote: 'Mr Rossiter ... fits the requirements perfectly' and added: '*Rising Damp* has a lot to commend it. Also in the cast are Richard Beckinsale, a young actor with a proven talent for TV comedy, and former Royal Shakespeare Company actress Frances de la Tour. Frances has demonstrated her comic ability too.'

John Duncan feels a lot of the programme's success was due to Leonard Rossiter. 'He was a brilliant actor, and I don't think he could have failed at anything. He was a meticulous, calculating performer.'

Eric is equally complimentary about Rossiter's role in the show's popularity. 'He was a very energetic performer who acted with his whole body. His performance was always a choreographed piece of work. He acted with every fibre of his being and at such a pace, too.' Many of Rossiter's screen portrayals were based on pace: quick reactions and a speed of movement both physical and verbal. 'I remember actors who were appearing in an episode saying how much they were looking forward to being on the show, but within a day or two they were going pale because of the demands thrust upon them. The speed of the production was partly due to the tight schedules but also because of the rate at which Leonard worked.'

Working with Rossiter on nineteen episodes, Ronnie Baxter was impressed by the actor's ability to get his teeth into the character early on. 'Leonard was so with it he would show you the whole performance very early, meaning I could prepare the camera script earlier than normal. He always knew exactly what he was going to do, which is a tribute to his professionalism.'

When considering the question of whether Rossiter created the Rigsby he'd envisaged, Eric is undecided. 'I think so, but it's hard thinking back to what I pictured before Len came on the scene. All I know is that he played the character beautifully and in the end I was writing for Len and Rigsby. At times he would say: "Rigsby would never do that, Eric." Here was the actor telling the writer, who's created the character, what he would and wouldn't do!'

While Rossiter's face was familiar to viewers, Don Warrington's was new. Fresh out of drama school when offered the role on stage, he made the transition to the small screen with ease. Eric admires Don for taking such matters in his stride. 'He was brave: imagine being pitched into a show like *Rising Damp* with all these highly talented, passionate professionals. He was learning the trade as he went along, and the pure fact that he came into the show and survived says much for his guts and determination. Apart from Len, Don turned out to be the only actor who appeared in every episode.'

Eric was happy with the way Don portrayed his character. 'One of his strengths was the ability to play an upper-crust, well-bred gentleman, which helped enormously. Don played a rather aloof man who was world-weary, qualities which we wanted. He got it together and did well: so well that people began imitating him by saying: "Hello, Rigsby" in Philip's style of voice. When people start doing that, you know you've made a success of the part.'

Equally enamoured was Ronnie Baxter. 'Don was very good and was learning a lot as the episodes went along. It was certainly an experience for him, especially working in the company of such great actors.'

When it comes to discussing Frances de la Tour, Eric believes she made the part her own. 'Miss Jones was the most underwritten part and it got better because of Frances. In the end, as I got to know the character and actress better, I was able to feed her the lines she could use so perfectly, especially with the quaint coyness she adopted. Miss Jones was probably the most difficult to write, but I'm very pleased with how she turned out, largely because of Frances.'

'Yes, I agree, she caught the character wonderfully,' adds Ronnie. 'She is such an experienced actress; it couldn't have been a better cast. She was wonderful and played against Leonard just right. It may sound dull to keep saying things like that, but it's true.'

John Duncan wasn't alone in thinking *The Banana Box* was suited to the small screen. David Isaacs, reviewing the play for the *Coventry Evening Telegraph* on its opening at Leicester's Phoenix Theatre in 1971, wrote: 'One could not help having the feeling from time to time ... that this was a television series – admittedly a very good one – which had somehow been delivered to the theatre by mistake.' He acknowledged this could be due in part to the fact that Wilfrid Brambell, of *Steptoe* fame, was playing one of the characters, but added: 'One feels, nevertheless, that the whole situation and the characters created in this play would be well suited to a comedy series on the small screen.'

The television sitcom retained the basic elements and themes of its theatrical forerunner, although its overall tone and attitudes were softened. It explored attitudes towards prejudices, but contained less of the play's darker side.

CHANGING NAMES

It wasn't until the show transferred to the small screen that the main character's name was changed. As Eric explains: 'We were just about to make the sitcom when Leonard Rossiter was interviewed by one of the national papers. At that stage the character was going to be called Rooksby on television, and Leonard said something like: "If you didn't like Hitler you certainly aren't going to like Rooksby." It made him sound like an absolute fascist, and a guy called Rooksby read it and wasn't very pleased. So I had a last-minute phone call from Duncan Wood at Yorkshire telling me I had to change the name. Once this man had objected we couldn't run with it.' Desperate for an alternative name, Eric turned to the local telephone directory and thumbed through the pages hunting for a name that, at least, sounded similar. He ended up with Rigsby. 'It seemed a bit of a poor substitute,' admits Eric, 'but now no one would think Rooksby was a good idea because Rigsby is firmly implanted in the mind.'

As a consequence of changing the central character's name, Eric decided he needed to alter the title of the sitcom. 'Changing the name to Rigsby got me thinking about the name of the show; somehow it no longer seemed appropriate to call it *The Banana Box*.' He put on his thinking cap. 'Because the house was supposed to be heavy and run-down, I tried coming up with the most depressing phrase in the English language and decided on *Rising Damp*. Wanting a second opinion, I sent my choice of name to Len Rossiter and he liked it; he loved anything of the macabre or sombre that was funny. He never played soft comedy, so he thought the name was ideal – and I stuck with it, although, I must admit, I remained unsure about it for some time. I thought: "My God, I know what the critics are going to do with this title." But Len kept saying: "Let's keep it, it's so funny." And the director for the pilot, Ian MacNaughton, must have spotted the danger signs in my eyes because he told me the Graphics Department had finished the credits and it was too late to change. I suppose I was suffering writer's nerves!'

With hindsight Eric realizes the title couldn't have been better suited to the show. 'It was absolutely perfect,' he says, 'but I didn't think so at the time, particularly when some people, like my father, commented: "It doesn't sound very good to me." There was one critic who wrote: "I saw *Rising Damp* the other night and thought it a little wet." But in the main the pressmen greeted it with enthusiasm, which was pleasing.'

DEVELOPING CHARACTERS

Rigsby was a bigot, of that there is no doubt. Some may even call him a racist. In having him refer repeatedly to Philip's ancestry, even though the black lodger was born in Croydon, Eric ran the risk of having his sitcom branded as containing too much racial material. Interestingly

Rising Damp on Stage

Just before Leonard Rossiter died, Eric Chappell was in discussion about a stage version of his sitcom. The play would have been based on the series, with an injection of fresh material. 'Ray Cooney, who has produced so many plays, had the idea of doing a *Rising Damp* play in the West End. As his guest, I went up to see one of his farces and Leonard was there, so too was Jimmy Bolam, who I think was going to play one of the characters. Len and Frances, I believe, had agreed to do it, and once everything had been sorted out I would go away and revise *The Banana Box.*

'Len went on to appear in *Loot* and it was during the production that he died. Obviously his death meant the idea for the play was dropped, but we nearly had a stage version of *Rising Damp*, and I was simply waiting for someone to give me the go-ahead to write the script – it was that close.'

enough, the programme received very little adverse publicity. Eric believes there is a simple reason for that. 'Philip, who was the butt of Rigsby's prejudices, always got the better of the exchanges with his land-lord. However, Don would never have played the part if he felt it was patronizing. Philip was more of a gentleman than Rigsby and all the misconceptions were kicked into touch. But Rigsby didn't like anyone, except Miss Jones; he didn't even like the bloke next door!

'Meeting people of a different race was a new experience for many people back in the 1960s and 1970s, and everyone was having to make adjustments. So I dealt with the subject in a light-hearted way. But you must remember that the original idea was about a man posing as the son of a chief; with Philip and Rigsby you have two flawed characters and that's what the show was about. Now and again, people ask how I got away with it, and maybe today sensitivities have grown to such an extent you daren't say anything about race. But people still find the show perfectly acceptable, so there can't have been much wrong with it. I feel we must not dodge issues and pretend they are not there because we are writing comedy about life. We're saying laugh at it, don't submit to it.'

Director Ronnie Baxter never gave the concern of racial criticism one thought. 'I think most sensible people took it for what it was: a comedy series where the man with all the opinions and views falls flat on his face every time. Most people thought Rigsby was a berk, and his arguments always came crashing down around him anyway. There was always tit for tat between him and Philip, and that's the way to do comedy. Philip always gave as good as he got. Don Warrington never objected to anything and nor did anyone else as far as I know.'

When Eric established the character of Miss Jones for his stage play *The Banana Box*, he was exploring new territory because he'd never created a female character before. With *Rising Damp* his characters would be exposed to his biggest audience yet, as they tuned in to see the transmission of the pilot episode on 2 September 1974. He realized that if a series was commissioned the characters would evolve as the sitcom progressed, but admits initially underwriting the part of Miss Jones. 'I think Frances felt this and commented that the part was a bit light,' he recalls. When the director contacted him one day because the third script, 'A Night Out', needed extending, Eric grasped the opportunity to write an additional scene involving Ruth: it turned out to be a key moment in the character's development.

'Ronnie Baxter said they needed a couple more pages of script,' says Eric. 'At first, I didn't know what to do, but whilst thumbing through a magazine, I saw an advert for a company selling scents and perfumes whose secrets were known only by women; I thought it was a great line.' The episode focused on Ruth's birthday and Eric wrote an extra scene in which Rigsby presented her with a bottle of perfume called Ritual in the Dark, together with plenty of embellishments, before mistaking one of her false eyelashes for a spider and stamping on it. The scene worked well. 'Someone described it as a "magic scene" and asked why I didn't write more like that. So I did, not that they took much writing, because Len and Frances were so good most of the humour came from their acting; even the way they looked at each other made for perfect comedy.'

The role of Miss Jones grew as a result of Eric's growing confidence and Frances de la Tour's acting abilities. 'She was a classical actress who came into my sitcom and must have wondered what she'd got herself involved in, but she played the part beautifully.'

As far as the remaining characters were concerned, the only one needing an overhaul was Noel Parker, who became Alan Moore on TV.

'The change of name seems to indicate a little more grittiness,' says Eric. 'The character in the play was priggish and quite religious, whereas Alan in the sitcom was innocent, even though he tried making out he wasn't.'

Explaining why the character was altered when the stage play took on a new identity for TV, Eric says: 'When you write a sitcom the comedic problems are different: you have to be funnier and more upfront, and I think Noel may have been too prissy for television. You also have to give your characters more range: you can't take just one facet and make a lot of it; they need to have several which are strong enough on which to base storylines. I wanted to write a sitcom which had a bit more muscular quality and felt the character needed developing.'

Eric was pleased with how Alan Moore turned out, but feels Richard Beckinsale wasn't too sure. 'He always argued that the character was one-dimensional. It wasn't a character he loved; he was marking time a bit because he'd already played an innocent young man in *The Lovers*.' It was clear to Eric that Richard wanted his career to move on. 'I always said he was a page waiting to be written on by life. He kept telling me how he wanted to play more mature, sophisticated parts, and I remember saying to him: "You don't need to rush and should enjoy the more innocent roles if that's what you're being offered – after all, there is plenty of time for everything else." Sadly, there wasn't. He was impatient about playing more mature roles, which is something that would have happened if he'd lived long enough, I'm certain about that.'

REHEARSALS

Although the sitcom was recorded at Yorkshire Television's studios in Leeds, rehearsals took place in West London, at the Sulgrave Boys' Club in Shepherd's Bush, except the first series, which was rehearsed at St Paul's Church Hall in nearby Hammersmith. Eric always attended rehearsals if possible, an experience he initially compared to sitting the eleven-plus! 'In later years I involved myself more, but in the beginning was slightly detached from proceedings. When it came to recording an episode I got very nervous because I didn't think the audience would enjoy it, but they always did.'

The genre of comedy writing usually dictates a more hands-on stance from the writer during rehearsals, as Eric explains. 'As a comedy writer you're involved more because if a line doesn't work in a comedic sense, you've got to go back to the writer. In drama, lines can be said in various ways, but in comedy if you want something to be funny it's got to be said in a certain way. You don't do something else while you're saying a funny line because it will distract; all these things you know instinctively if you write comedy. Sometimes an actor can't get a line to work, so I have to alter it or we talk about it. So the writer ought to be there, simply because he's asking for a certain reaction from the audience and if it's not coming, something has to be done about it.'

THE AUDIENCE

While some actors quiver at the thought of recording a sitcom in front of a studio audience, most writers and producers believe it's an essential part in the making of a series. *Rising Damp* was recorded in Leeds in front of a studio audience and Eric advocates this procedure. 'I've always felt you need an audience for sitcoms. A good one will pinpoint where you have done well or timed to perfection, but they'll also let you know if the pace of the show is too slow. For the actor, the audience will certainly let them know when they've got it right, and it's a magical moment when you trigger that response. I'm not saying you can't write a successful show without people watching, it's just that I always regard an audience as a tutor.'

The Theme Tune

When Eric Chappell first heard the theme tune chosen for the series, he described it as 'very ordinary'. Producer Duncan Wood told him it had to be simple because that way it would be remembered. It soon became one of most memorable television theme tunes of all time. The tune was written by the late Dennis Wilson, a top British pianist for many years. He wrote much background music and provided signature tunes and incidental music for top shows, including *Marriage Lines*, *Till Death Us Do Part*, *My Wife Next Door*, *Fawlty Towers*, *You're Only Young Twice*, *Life Begins at Forty*, *Not in Front of the Children*, *Here's Harry*, *Seven Faces of Jim*, *Scott On...*, *Second Time Around*, *Steptoe and Son* (incidental music only), *Misleading Cases* and *Three Piece Suite*.

Dennis Wilson died in 1989 after a series of strokes.

Vernon Lawrence, who directed the fourth series, also believes that it's beneficial to record a sitcom in front of a studio audience, but acknowledges the difficulty it can give performers. 'The actors need this terrific discipline to cope with cameras, but while they're performing for the cameras they can also see and hear the audience. However trained you are, you can be completely thrown by an audience which finds something hilariously funny when you hadn't expected it.

'Overall I think it helps enormously, especially if you've got an experienced cast. If you've got someone who's inexperienced they occasionally raise the size of their performance and if you're not careful you end up with a gross performance, particularly in the less successful sitcoms. Actors grope for laughs and they think the only thing to do is play large by doing a stage portrayal which ruins the actual size of performance you need for television.'

But actors have Vernon's utmost respect because he appreciates audiences are always unpredictable. 'If you do a comedy in the theatre you've probably been out on the road for anything between six and eleven weeks, working it round the country. When you come into the West End you're ninety-five per cent sure you know where the laughs will come. With a sitcom your first exposure to an audience is also your last – you only have one crack at it.'

THE FIRST EPISODE

The pilot episode of *Rising Damp*, 'The New Tenant' (also known as 'Rooksby') was transmitted on 2 September 1974, the first of six new half-hour comedies from Yorkshire Television. Duncan Wood had faith in the show, telling a journalist it was 'definitely series material'. Even though Eric had had concerns about certain aspects of its forerunner, he could only have felt joy and satisfaction with his first attempt at a television sitcom. Producing a compact, fast-paced half-hour script like 'The New Tenant' boded well for his future in the genre. Usually it takes time for viewers to understand and form an opinion on television characters, but with *Rising Damp* it seemed as if you'd known Rigsby, Ruth, Philip and Alan for some while.

Eric describes watching the screening of the pilot episode as a 'big thrill', but admits such pleasant thoughts were quickly dispelled by his self-confessed pessimism. 'I've been known for it for years,' he admits, 'so while I was watching the pilot I was also thinking: "Yes, it's all right, but what about the next one?"' He kept trying to convince himself that the ability he'd shown in writing the script for 'The New Tenant' wasn't just a flash in the pan. 'The audience watching the recording of the pilot loved it, and Leonard was superb. I remember saying to friends: "I think we're home and dry with this." But you still have to write the other episodes, and even when the first series is successful, you have to write the next. I was always living in fear that scripts would be returned because someone at Yorkshire didn't like them. Luckily that didn't happen with *Rising Damp*, but the first radio play I wrote after turning to full-time writing was sent back; they let me keep the first part of the advance but scrapped the play – it was demoralizing.'

The pilot was warmly welcomed by the critics, who were particularly impressed by Rossiter's performance. Journalist Ken Burgess wrote: 'He lightly flicks away his best lines with a quick lick of the lips, and a faint narrowing of the eyes.' Burgess added that as long as the series concentrated on Rossiter all would be well.

Fellow journalist James Thomas felt *Rising Damp* was 'very funny'. He believed the programme was 'one of the best comedy shows to come off the commercial screens for some time.' Peter Fiddick, meanwhile, felt the show would make a welcome series if 'it keeps up to the same standards of hard work and quiet inventiveness' as shown by the pilot.

Although many journalists singled out Rossiter for much of the praise received by the pilot episode, the other three actors and the producer, Ian MacNaughton, whose previous credits included *Monty Python*, received their fair share of plaudits. While journalist Sylvia Clayton wrote: 'Ian MacNaughton ... directed this pilot programme with confident attack', Patrick Campbell also felt Ian deserved some of the credit, stating: 'Without Ian MacNaughton's direction, walking the tightrope between comedy and farce and hardly faltering, Leonard Rossiter's performance might have stood alone, instead of being carefully blended into the four-handed teamwork.'

Ian, who also helped produce the series *Q* with Spike Milligan, had worked for Duncan Wood several times at the BBC. As a freelance director he was interested when Duncan asked him to work on the pilot episode. 'I thought the script was very funny,' he says. 'It was so good I knew it would make a series.' He felt the script contained two components essential for situation comedy: realistic characters and human conflict. 'I recognized the landlord, Rigsby, immediately; I'd been an actor myself for years and lived in digs all over the place, so it wasn't difficult putting a human touch to him.'

When the series was commissioned, Ian wasn't available to direct it, but when he did join the team a facet of his own experience helped him to relate to Alan: 'I studied medicine for nine months in 1941 and had experienced many of the issues of student life. Richard Beckinsale was marvellous; he wasn't just a foil for Leonard, he was a very good comic.' Ian went on to work with Leonard in the short film *Le Pétomane*, and was always impressed with his performances. 'Leonard had perfect timing and was tremendous fun to work with, and so was Frances. But the show was full of wonderful conflicts: Rigsby adoring Miss Jones, who in turn likes Philip, so Rigsby is jealous of Philip – all these situations were classic set-ups for situation comedy.'

Eric was also pleased with how the pilot went, and after reading the glowing newspaper reviews was a little more confident the sitcom could be a success, especially with Rossiter in the lead role. 'As soon as I saw Len with the studio audience I knew that as long as I could maintain a reasonable standard of writing, we were home and dry.' On the strength of the pilot, he was commissioned to write further episodes, although it was a protracted affair, as he recalls: 'Duncan Wood commissioned very slowly, he was a very crafty guy. After one show he'd say: "Do you want to do another one?" Then two more, and we crept through the first series until we finally completed seven shows.'

THE FOUR SERIES

The early scripts for the first series drew heavily on *The Banana Box* and it wasn't until the fifth episode that Eric used new material. 'I fed off the play because I didn't have many ideas,' he admits. But he reached a point with 'All Our Yesterdays', in which Rigsby reminisced about his war years, where he realized he could write a series and not just cannibalize the play. 'I kept telling myself that if I write one, I could write another. From then on, I knew I could take a subject and write about it. I had the characters, the set-up, and if I was stuck I could introduce a new person to the scene – perhaps another lodger, an actor, a suicide or two lovers. Then all I have to think about is what Rigsby, Alan, Philip or Ruth would say about it. You'd end up with vignettes showing their reactions, before even thinking about how the characters would react together. The plots, although never easy, would be more manageable.'

A Cat's Life

They say a man's best friend is his dog, but for Rigsby it was his black and white cat, Vienna. Since separating from his wife, Veronica, Rigsby has lived alone with his moggy, with whom he shares his secrets and frustrations, often with the help of a quick boot! But despite his intermittent cruelty, Rigsby thinks the world of Vienna and while she always gets the best cat food, she's also allowed the occasional indulgence, like licking the dinner plates before they are washed.

Eric Chappell decided Rigsby would have a cat for specific reasons. 'A lot of lonely people have cats, and it gave someone for Rigsby to talk to whenever he was on his own, which is what I needed.' The scriptwriter admits that Vienna and Leonard Rossiter never saw eye to eye. 'Although he was fond of cats, he didn't really get along with Vienna. The cat didn't seem to like acting, especially with Len, and he always told me how she smelt of fish.'

Stage manager Terry Knowles agrees. 'The cat didn't like Len. Whenever he got hold of her, she used to go rigid and fart a lot! Len would say: "This cat's done it again."'

Filming with animals can be hair-raising and unpredictable, as Knowles knows from experience. 'Whenever we were using Vienna in the studio the handler had to keep hold of her all the time; I remember on a couple of occasions she got loose and scooted under the audience rostra and wouldn't come out.' Recording was sometimes halted for up to fifteen minutes while members of the production team tried coaxing her out. Thanks to Leonard, the cat changed its sex during the run of the sitcom. 'Over the years Len would refer to it as a female, other times as a tom cat, so I'm not too sure what sex it was.' Away from the screen, Vienna was in fact a female cat called Katie, later to be replaced by Patsy, a rescue cat owned by Jean Lister.

Vienna Mark I, which made her debut in the pilot, was predominantly white, while the replacement, who first graced our screens in 'Great Expectations', was mainly black. The first cat was owned by Peggy Sample, who worked as bookkeeper and secretary in a Leeds veterinary surgery after retiring from Barclays Bank. A spinster all her life, Peggy adored cats and at one point owned eighteen. She eventually moved to North Wales but died in 1995, aged eighty-two. The strays she took in and cared for must have thought they had arrived at a five-star hotel because they were always fed the best: salmon, chicken breast, liver and beef were often on the menu.

Peggy's nephew, illustrator and artist Paul Sample, remembers visiting his aunt when she lived with her cats in a Leeds flat. 'I remember opening her fridge and finding it packed with cat food, nothing else. And I remember one of the cats scratching me while I held it, but instead of telling it off, Peggy sided with the cat and blamed me!' Working with animals can cause chaos if you're not careful; although Vienna's performances were largely uneventful, director Vernon Lawrence was witness to the cat's occasional wilfulness. 'She was always well looked after, but cats like treading their own path, don't like television studios, don't like television light and don't like audiences, but Eric insisted on writing the creature into the scripts – he didn't have to work with it. All animals are a nuisance to work with, and you can see Len having to hold it quite firmly sometimes. It used to scratch him. Vienna was a great character and very useful, but I always flinched when I saw it in the script.' The owner of Vienna Mark II was Jean Lister, a friend of Peggy Sample and coordinator of an animal welfare charity. Patsy was one of nine cats cared for by Jean. About eight years old when she made her appearance in series four, Patsy was given her chance of stardom when Peggy couldn't continue with the job. Jean's daughter, Caroline Cardis, recalls: 'We didn't get any money for it, but mother was happy to help out. Patsy was a very placid cat and lived for some five years after appearing on television. I remember she ran under the raised studio set on one occasion; to try and keep her from wandering, my mother put butter on the cat's feet, and also used her blanket on Rigsby's sofa, which helped her to settle down.'

Although we never see a dog in the series, Rigsby mentions Vienna is chasing 'the dog' around the back garden during 'The Last of the Big Spenders'. When Brenda believes Rigsby wants to take her out for a slap-up meal, he suggests they eat in because Vienna's under the weather. He's later forced to change his mind, and when Brenda enquires about the cat's health, Rigsby explains she's made a rapid recovery and is out chasing 'the dog'.

One of the major developments within the sitcom was the departure of Frances de la Tour during the second series. After falling in love with the bespectacled mummy's boy Desmond, who worked at the local library, Miss Jones bowed out in the fourth episode and sought new horizons with her fiancé. Frances left to work in the theatre, an engagement she was due to move on to once the second run of *Rising Damp* had been recorded; however, when the recording schedule was delayed, it meant she was unable to do the final three episodes and the Christmas Special because the play had already started.

The delay in recording was due to the fact that Eric was unable to cope with the workload. 'I was writing two series a year – *Rising Damp* and *The Squirrels* – and just couldn't manage,' he explains. 'I didn't have a nervous breakdown or anything dramatic, I just couldn't do it in time. It got to the point where I threw the pen down and said: "I can't do any more."' He spent too long on *The Squirrels*, eating into time set aside for the second series of *Rising Damp*. To compound the problem, he was told production was being brought forward, leaving him with four scripts to write in a month. 'It was ludicrous because in those days it took me about three weeks to write one script.'

The distillation process, from dreaming up an idea for an episode to typing the final word of the script, lasted approximately three weeks. It was an arduous period. 'I did a lot of writing at that time: I completed about three drafts before the final version,' says Eric. 'So if you think about it, each episode took three weeks to write, a week to rehearse, one and a half hours to record, and went out in just over twenty-four minutes – what a reduction in time.'

To ease the pressure, other writers were drafted in to complete scripts for *The Squirrels*, while Eric concentrated on *Rising Damp*. 'I wasn't going to let *Rising Damp* go to other writers; I was determined to keep control of that programme, even if I had to stop writing *The Squirrels*.' The decision he made was the right one, and he went on to complete scripts for *Rising Damp*, maintaining the same degree of quality as he had put into the previous series.

Less robust sitcoms facing the void left behind by a key character's departure would have crumbled, but *Rising Damp* marched on, a remarkable feat when you consider the main cast was now reduced to just three performers. The show had the mettle to cope with the change, and its continued success under strenuous circumstances proved that Eric had created a top-class show. 'It was a blow to lose Frances,' he says, 'but there was nothing we could do about it. We brought another actress in, Gay Rose, who played Brenda, and it worked well, so Frances leaving didn't actually set us back too much.'

Finding the right slot in the TV schedules meant the programme didn't establish itself immediately. 'The sitcom wasn't publicized much and didn't have a prime-time slot, so it took a while before we established a decent following,' explains Eric, and it wasn't until the end of the second series that *Rising Damp* crept in to the Top Twenty. The programme didn't attract big audiences at first, but there was a moment when the writer knew his sitcom was going to become a hit show. During a dress rehearsal he noticed technicians and office staff starting to drop in, and within minutes almost seventy people had gathered to watch the show. It looked as if the audience had arrived early. 'These were people working in the industry who had seen it all, and here they were enjoying my show,' he says. 'They started getting tickets and bringing their families to watch the recording; it was then I realized that if professionals liked it, it must be good.'

Rising Damp returned to the screens with a third series in November 1977, nearly two years after the Christmas Special, 'For the Man Who Has Everything'. The delay in recording the third season was due to Leonard Rossiter's contractual commitment to film *The Fall and Rise of Reginald Perrin*, and Frances de la Tour being pregnant with her son.

The new series marked the return of Miss Jones, which pleased Eric. 'Frances was part of the chemistry. It was good because the first episode, "That's My Boy", virtually wrote itself, with Miss Jones's return being the main focus.'

The difficulties Eric encountered during the previous series were now behind him and he felt more assured when it came to writing the seven scripts for the new season. 'Usually the third series of any show goes well because it's established itself with viewers. I found it easier to think up plots for these episodes, and I was probably reaching my peak in terms of generating ideas.'

The third series saw the house opened up to other unfortunates who happened to eke out a miserable existence in Rigsby's dispiriting abode. Although their televisual life was brief, the characters seen during the season widened the scope as far as storylines were concerned; there were more comedic opportunities at Eric's disposal. He had explored this idea in an earlier episode, 'A Perfect Gentleman', with Henry McGee playing Seymour, the guileful rogue, but now a string of lodgers brought a new dimension to five instalments in the series. Mrs Brent arrived clutching a baby in 'That's My Boy', the 'resting' thespian, Hilary, introduced his own drama to 'Stage Struck', while the manic-depressive Mr Gray brought an air of gloom to the house in 'The Good Samaritans'. And before the series closed, we'd also met the busty erotic dancer Marilyn, together with her pet python, and the world's greatest hypochondriac, Osborne. 'Although the main characters were interesting in themselves, I'd explored them thoroughly by this time,' says Eric. 'We were always needing new situations for Rigsby and the others to react against, and it was fortunate that I could simply open the door and bring in someone new.'

Two important changes affected the fourth and final series: Richard Beckinsale left and direction was handed over to Vernon Lawrence when Ronnie Baxter moved to work on *In Loving Memory*. Richard was involved in a play in London and was not free to continue the role of Alan. Although Frances's absence in the latter stages of series two was made less painful by introducing a new character, Brenda (played by Gay Rose), Richard's absence from the starting line-up was more difficult to manage, partly because his room-mate, Philip, no longer had anyone to bounce off. The banter and tête-à-têtes which took place between the assured, confident, worldly-wise Philip and the naïve, callow Alan were highly amusing and valuable to the programme; losing Richard created, in many people's eyes, an unbridgeable chasm, and some serious thinking was required in order to maintain the standard set by the preceding series.

'Alan and Philip were always talking about Rigsby,' says Eric, who was only too aware of the predicament. 'A lot of people loved the conversations between the two students, so we lost something.' Whereas earlier he had replaced Frances with another female character, retaining some of the magic, the loss of Richard was more of a headache. 'I actually thought to myself: "Thank heavens we're only doing one more series."' One way he addressed the problem was to introduce new characters, around which an episode would be based, something he had tried out in the third series. In 'Hello Young Lovers', Robin and Lorna rented a room, while the religious freak Gwyn Williams arrived on the scene in 'Fire and Brimstone'. But Eric still feels uneasy about the outcome: 'We lost something and as a result the fourth series was weak.'

Vernon Lawrence, who joined Yorkshire Television from the BBC in 1973, doesn't agree and feels Eric 'coped admirably well'. 'I was sad Richard wasn't in the series because I had worked with him on other projects, and the onus fell on Eric because he suddenly lost one of his major characters. But he handled the dilemma and Don Warrington was given much more to do.' Don's greater involvement helped the sitcom through what turned out to be another successful season. 'He did very well and was a breath of fresh air,' says Vernon. 'He was a talented guy playing a brilliant character: Philip was articulate, educated and deeply intelligent; it went very much against the grain of the political feelings at that time, and Don played him beautifully with that wonderful cut-glass voice.'

Rising Damp was to win a BAFTA for Best Comedy, a proud moment for everyone involved in the show, and Eric Chappell attended his first award ceremony on 12 March 1975, at London's Café Royal. The Writers' Guild of Great Britain had selected *Rising Damp* as a contender for the coveted title of Best British Comedy Script. It would be competing with three other sitcoms: *It Ain't Half Hot, Mum, Last of the Summer Wine* and *Porridge*. Eric's sitcom was pipped to the post by *Porridge* and voted runner-up. He still has vivid memories of the event: 'It was all so strange. I was asked by executives at Yorkshire Television to be their guest at an awards ceremony, simply because they felt I'd been a successful writer for them during the year.'

Eric and his wife were booked into an opulent suite at a top-class hotel, and attended the event dressed to the nines. 'I felt totally out of my depth,' he admits. 'It's funny how these things happen to you; suddenly I was in this crowd at the Café Royal, and it was full of luminaries. I looked around and knew every face, people like Les Dawson and Ronnie Barker – famous people. I stood there and couldn't believe that I was part of all this. When I picked up one of the programmes I suddenly saw *Rising Damp* was a nominated show, but no one had told me. It was a proud moment.'

Looking back over the past two decades in the history of television sitcom, most of the shows which have survived into the twenty-first century and are regarded as 'classics' are BBC-produced, but Yorkshire Television's *Rising Damp* is a glowing exception. Vernon feels there are a host of reasons why it has been so successful. 'It stands up incredibly well in the same way as *Steptoe and Son* because it has got basic truths with which the audience can identify; the characters' attitudes are also clearly defined, and were expertly played out by the actors. Watching Len and Frances rehearse was magical: they admired each other's talents, helped each other and were absolutely terrific, and so was Don.'

THE BEST AND WORST

When it comes to selecting favourite episodes, Eric has no problems listing his top three. 'I like "The Permissive Society" because it was a departure from the play and gave me a boost of confidence, "Stage Struck" with Peter Bowles and "Clunk Click". They're the episodes that stand out in my mind.' Deciding on his least favourite is more difficult. 'It's probably "A Night Out", partly because Len was very nervous about it. He never thought it was as good as the others because we'd left the house. We lost the claustrophobic element because the restaurant was a big set and everything was spread out. If you're not careful, when you've got a bigger space to fill you can lose comedy. But it worked well and many people view it as their favourite, although I don't regard it as such, purely because of Len's reaction.'

As director of the fourth series, Vernon Lawrence enjoyed most the final episode, 'Come On In, the Water's Lovely', in which Rigsby at last plucks up enough courage to propose to his long-term love, Miss Jones. 'Although he asks, he's expecting a negative response, so throws the ring away. But, of course, she accepts. It's a very funny scene. I also like the scene where he ends up going to the wrong church. It's a brilliant episode.'

As far as the other directors are concerned, Len Lurcuck feels 'Things That Go Bump in the Night' is one of the best, while Ronnie Baxter opts for 'Stage Struck'. 'I could sit down now and watch that one,' he enthuses. 'That was the submitted episode which won us the BAFTA in 1977. I remember having a chat with Duncan Wood and Eric Chappell and we all agreed "Stage Struck" should be chosen to represent *Rising Damp*.'

It's reported that Leonard Rossiter's favourite episode was 'Clunk Click'.

CLOSING THE DOOR AT RIGSBY'S

Bringing a sitcom to an end, particularly one as successful as *Rising Damp*, is never an easy decision, but it was one Eric was determined to make. After writing the final line for the script 'Come On In, the Water's Lovely', he called it a day, even though the fourth series contained just six episodes instead of the normal seven. 'I was never going to write a fifth series; Richard had already left the cast and Len wouldn't have done it. He always said that if he wanted to be in a long-running show he'd have stayed at the insurance office. There was never any question about continuing, and I've never regretted the decision, even though writing more would have made me a lot of money.

'Len and I both felt we had other things to do. We didn't want to hang around until people got fed up with us – although considering the success of *Last of the Summer Wine*, we could have probably carried on for another two years if we hadn't had ambitions in other directions.' Eric felt a need to prove to himself that he could write another sitcom. 'I had written *The Squirrels* but dropped out of that, so the pessimist within forced me to write a third show: I couldn't stay with a successful sitcom, I had to do another.' He needn't have questioned his talent because his following sitcom, *Only When I Laugh*, became a bigger hit than *Rising Damp* in terms of audience figures.

Lawrence was sad the fourth season was going to be the last. 'Personally I was sorry because I'd only done one series, but in hindsight I think the great joy was that we got out on top. We all walked away from a thumping great hit; doing that is very brave and on reflection you ask yourself: "Could we have done another one, another two, maybe?", but then the history of British comedy is littered with people who have gone on and made too many shows.'

Stage versus TV

'I thought the TV series was very good,' says Stephen MacDonald, who directed *The Banana Box*. 'Beckinsale and Rossiter were marvellous, Warrington was different but very good and Frances de la Tour was almost as good as Janet Michael but not quite, in my view. Frances didn't play the character with the touch of faint hysteria like Janet, but it still worked well. The sitcom was different as far as television was concerned, but more than anything else I was glad to see that Eric had got away from the electricity board.'

What the Papers Said

'It is marked as a winner straight away.'

Gerard Dempsey, *Daily Express*

'Oh precious stuff!'

William Marshall, *Daily Mirror*

'Leonard Rossiter is worth a quarter-mile start to any comedy show.'

Shaun Usher, *Daily Mail*

'There are so many factors that make it a paragon of funnies . . .'

Tom Holt, *The Stage*

'The sort of professional performances that just make you purr.'

Peter Fiddick, *Guardian*

'Leonard Rossiter's Mr Rigsby, keeper of a seedy boarding house catering mainly for students, established himself at once as a memorable personality.'

Sylvia Clayton, *Daily Telegraph*

'Magic from the word go...'

Chris Watson, *Western Daily Press* (Bristol)

'Leonard Rossiter's bragging conceited Rigsby is a precisely conceived role superbly executed.'

Stewart Lane, *Morning Star*

'The series has been a personal triumph for the versatile and hardworking Leonard Rossiter. He plays it so frantically at times that it seems he'll spoil everything by going right over the top. But he knows just what he is doing and always stops short of a hair's breadth.'

James Thomas, *Daily Express*

'Well, there was certainly a seeping wetness about this programme last night. But what else can one say about this situation comedy now squeezed out into a series?'

Leonard Buckley, *The Times*

Like all genuine classics, episodes of *Rising Damp* are just as accessible and enjoyable today, over two decades later, than when they were originally transmitted. But one person who doesn't make a point of watching repeats is the show's creator. 'It's all right for the producer and the actors to watch repeats, but if the writer does he often finds himself writing the same material again because the words stick in your mind. You have to move on. Occasionally I watch and enjoy it, but don't switch on every time it's repeated.'

When ruminating on the show's success, Eric feels it's partly because the show didn't instantly date itself by focusing on too many topical issues. He avoided the sitcom becoming too representative of a particular decade. 'There is nothing that dates faster than being too topical and *Rising Damp* wasn't. It also has a nostalgic quality: it tells you a little about the period of time, and in *Rising Damp*'s case that is the 1970s, or possibly the 1960s, when the idea was originally conceived. But we didn't follow the trends of the period too closely, which means people can relate to the show and find it amusing today.'

4

BRINGING THE SHOW TO LIFE

As with any other television programme, making a sitcom calls for a wide range of skills in the producer. Of paramount importance is the ability to plan and coordinate the coming together of many components, particularly with the sort of deadlines that faced *Rising Damp*. 'Each episode was basically made in three and a half days,' stresses producer Ronnie Baxter. While the episodes were recorded at Yorkshire Television's studios in Leeds, rehearsals took place in London, the most convenient location for the actors; as a result, part of the week was eaten up with travelling.

Even with a full week to produce an episode, the pressure is on, but this is intensified when you lose more time by being on the road, so it was just as well that Ronnie and Vernon Lawrence, director of the fourth series, could rely on Eric Chappell to deliver a script of quality which needed little, if any, editing. When Ronnie first heard the scripts being read, it was like music to his ears. 'It was like listening to a symphony; the scripts made a super read from day one, and it was marvellous hearing the output coming from the rehearsals.'

Designer Colin Pigott agrees, and for him one of the best aspects of the *Rising Damp* scripts was the absence of stage directions. 'I've worked on shows where the scripts contain, perhaps, three pages of stage directions, virtually telling you how to do your job. I can't see the point in that, but Eric's scripts were never like that. They were brilliantly constructed, and although they would change a little before being given to the actors, I can never remember any serious rewrites. They were astonishing to read, there was little you had to do to them. As soon as you picked up the script you knew you were on to something promising.'

Rigsby – the landlord from hell?

Alan studied medicine at the local university.

Miss Jones always had a soft spot for Philip.

Rigsby was constantly barging in on Philip and Alan, unannounced.

Rigsby grasped every moment to impress Miss Jones.

The repartee between Rigsby and his lodgers was a major factor in the show's success.

The insufferable Vienna, who changed colour during the life of the show.

Was this really one of Rigsby's previous tenants?

When Mr. Cooper (George A. Cooper) came ranting about the 'permissive society', Rigsby sent him packing with a flea in his ear.

Seymour (Henry McGee), the biggest fraudster in town, has the gullible Rigsby under his spell in 'The Perfect Gentleman'.

In the absence of Miss Jones, Brenda (Gay Rose) became the object of Rigsby's desires.

Spooner (the late Derek Newark)
appeared in two episodes.

Mrs Brent (Ann Beach)
arrived in 'That's My Boy'.

At first, the childless Rigsby wasn't too pleased with the new arrival.

A less than convincing doll was used in 'That's My Boy'.

In 'Stage Struck', Hilary (Peter Bowles) was on the look-out for acting talent.

SCHEDULES

Although the day of recording changed during the run (Sunday for the pilot and series one; Fridays thereafter) the schedule remained tight. One day would be spent plotting the episode and completing a read-through in London, during which several members of the production team would be involved as well as the actors, followed by two and a half days of rehearsals. Next the technical run, where the camera and sound crews are involved, takes place, at which point the scenes are acted out exactly as the show will be recorded. Everybody then travelled to Leeds and on the recording day the camera and dress rehearsals were followed by the actual recording in front of the audience.

The delivery of the week's script got the ball rolling in the production department, as Ronnie Baxter explains. 'When the scripts arrived, Duncan Wood, being in charge of the department, would read them; at the same time, I would look at them and discuss any particular points with Eric Chappell. Once transmission times had been agreed, rehearsal and studio times could be arranged, and from there everything else seemed to follow automatically.'

The next step was casting. With the show's regular artists already on board, guest roles and minor characters had to be recruited, but because of the sitcom's interior setting, very few additional artists were required. 'But we did use some extra people and at this point casting could take place; you can't contract artists until you've confirmed all the relevant dates,' Ronnie explains.

Budgets would need to be allocated for each department working on the show – including the design teams responsible for costumes and sets – while the read-through and rehearsal dates were confirmed. 'The read-through would always take place on Sunday at the rehearsal room in London,' recalls Ronnie. 'That was the first time the cast read the script together; other people from Wardrobe, Make-up and Design would be there to pick up on any requirements. They would then return to Leeds, leaving the rest of us to carry on with the rehearsals for the remainder of the day. Monday, Tuesday and Wednesday morning were also straight rehearsal days, but Wednesday afternoon was taken up with the technical run, with representatives from the camera and sound departments having arrived from Leeds.

'All the props we'd used during our rehearsals would be collected together, and the production team would catch the train up to Leeds, with the artists following on Thursday, ready for the studio rehearsal on Friday morning. Initially we would work with the cameras in the studio, gradually working through the day until about four o'clock, when we'd do the dress rehearsal. At that point everything was as we would record it later that night. After a little tea, the audience would come in half an hour before recording and we'd start shooting at 7.30pm. After recording, the artists would go back to their hotels, travel home on Saturday, and on Sunday we'd start all over again.'

IT'S ALL ABOUT TEAMWORK

Teamwork is the name of the game when you've only got a week to make a television show, and Ronnie Baxter can't speak highly enough of the team he assembled for *Rising Damp*. 'Everybody could be relied upon, they were true professionals,' the producer says. From Colin Pigott designing the sets to Linda Doyle, Ronnie's assistant, everyone pulled together to help make the sitcom a success. 'From top to bottom we had a good team; everywhere I looked I saw people who were good individually and as part of a team. People like Linda, who was my secretary and assistant. She worked mainly in the office, but held everything together whilst I was down in London. It was a wonderful team to have around me.'

DESIGNING THE SET

For a sitcom to work on television there are certain essential requirements: in addition to a strong, capable cast, scripts oozing quality and a good production team, it must have sets that complement the style and mood of the show. Opt for cheap, wobbly, unrealistic alternatives and viewers' attention is drawn away from the acting. By contrast, the sets depicting Rigsby's run-down boarding house couldn't have been more fitting.

One could have been forgiven for believing the television sets had been based on those used in *The Banana Box*, but as designer Colin Pigott points out, he never saw the show. 'I heard about it and would love to have seen it, but the style of sets I designed for the pilot, then redesigned when the first series was commissioned, were original.'

Born in Letchworth, Hertfordshire, Colin studied interior design for three years at Kingston School of Art. During the course he began to realize he wanted to work in television and on graduating he secured a job at the BBC as a holiday relief in the design department. In 1963 he was employed full-time and began assisting on productions like *Dr Finlay's Casebook*, before moving into light entertainment and shows including *The Black and White Minstrels* and *The Val Doonican Show*.

The first sitcom Colin worked on was *Marriage Lines*, followed by numerous other programmes, such as *Steptoe and Son* and *Harry Worth*. He left the BBC in 1967 and went freelance, working for various commercial channels, including London Weekend and Yorkshire, the latter association lasting nearly eighteen years. Colin continues to work as a freelance designer for all the major television stations.

After creating a plan for the sets, Colin met the producer, initially Duncan Wood and Ian MacNaughton for the pilot, and then Ronnie Baxter when the first series was commissioned. 'I made little models, and together with my ground plan and sketches, I would meet with the producer and discuss the sets. Both Duncan and Ronnie knew what they wanted. All designers have a particular fault: we design things too big, so Ronnie Baxter asked me to scale everything down, such as the beds in Alan and Philip's room. They wouldn't have fitted in them, but no one ever noticed because the camera was always at the end of the bed, or looking straight on.'

Another decision was to raise the sets eighteen inches off the ground. 'We felt it gave the actors an area to work within, almost like a stage, and it worked extremely well.'

Overall, Colin was given the freedom to design and create the sets in his own way. 'There was a trust between us; they all knew I'd worked on other things and must have liked what I'd done because they left it to me. I'd do some drawings, then make little models, before sitting down and working out the best way of shooting the scenes. The all-important thing in any situation comedy is to get everything right in its position, and with Ronnie Baxter the planning was very explicit. We didn't talk much about decoration – he left that to me. I showed him samples of wallpaper and colours, but decisions like that were mine. Ronnie always did his homework and planned meticulously, partly because he shot within inches of the edge of the set. We had a chippy on standby to actually cut bits off the set that we weren't seeing to give us more room. It still astonishes me how small the sets were, but they worked.'

The décor developed as the sitcom progressed. In the early episodes, Alan and Philip's room is noticeably uncluttered compared with later episodes, but one aspect that remained constant for the four series was the drab colouring running throughout the boarding house. 'We painted the sets very dark colours, so I'm glad I had someone as good as Peter Hardman lighting the set.' Colin didn't base the colour and design on anywhere he'd experienced in his own life. 'It was probably influenced, if anything, by being around Leeds in the sixties and seventies, because it was a pretty grim place then. A lot of houses had arched windows and strange attic rooms; they all looked incredibly damp, horrible and grey. Leeds has changed so much now, but back then we tried to catch something of the atmosphere, and Peter was hugely instrumental in achieving that by not overlighting the sets.

'Sets for comedy shows are generally overlit, but ours weren't. I remember the [ITV] Network complaining because they thought it was too dark for comedy, but we didn't want it to look like comedy, we wanted it to look real.'

The cheerless colours helped suggest a dingy house ridden with damp. 'I chose a lot of dark greens, which was a bit dangerous because green is unlucky as far as some theatrical people are concerned; there was a murmuring about the colour because you couldn't use green in television in those days because some actors wouldn't come on! I remember working on a series with an actress who got her manager to check there was no green anywhere before she came on the set. Plants were OK because they were natural, but nothing else was allowed. It was unbelievable.

'I also chose the browns and greens because I wanted the actors to stand out: you mustn't upstage the action that's going on, but people started asking me things like: "Where did you get the wallpaper in Miss Jones's room?" It was from Sanderson's actually, but it took days of work to make it look old and tatty. We used to blow it down with an air gun, and then use polish and all sorts of things to distress and age it – a normal technique in the industry. I wanted to make it so that no one would want to live there, but in the end people started liking it.'

From Colin's point of view, working in front of a live audience is disadvantageous to the designer. 'It's annoying because everything has to face the audience, and you always have to think of them, although I fully understand why such shows are recorded in this way.' But he enjoyed working on the series. 'It was fun, and I went on to work on most of Eric Chappell's shows, including *Only When I Laugh*, *The Bounder* and *Duty Free*.'

Colin and his team tried their utmost to work at least two episodes ahead, but it wasn't always possible bearing in mind the tight production schedules. 'I would sit in on the read-through and then leave them to it until the Wednesday, by which time the whole episode would be taking shape. Then it was set and lights day back up in Leeds on the Thursday, we'd record on the Friday, in most cases, and then Saturday was spent drawing next week's sets. Then on Sunday you were back to the next read-through. It was a bit relentless but once you've got your main sets built, everything can be made up within four days, so most times we were working a week ahead quite comfortably.'

From the moment Colin read the pilot script, he knew the series had potential. 'It was brilliant, and probably my favourite show to have worked on. Eric Chappell's scripts are beautifully constructed, and always arrived the correct weight,' he says. 'Today you get scripts half an inch too thick which have to be cut to bits in the studio, which is always embarrassing in front of actors. They also have to be rewritten as we're recording them. But hardly a word of Eric's needed changing.'

The designer sums up his experience on *Rising Damp* thus: 'There is nothing better than working on a top show. When you're working with good actors, a great script and you hear the audience laugh, there's nothing to beat that feeling; there was never a duff *Rising Damp* script, they were all classics. They were hysterically funny, exciting to do and worked like clockwork.'

Complementing the dowdy atmosphere conjured up by Colin's sets, another eye-grabbing aspect of the design is the tatty, old door that greets you as the opening and closing titles start to roll. First seen for the episode 'Charisma', it was shot half-length in order to occupy most of the space on the television screen. Graphic designer Ed Bailey didn't have to travel far when given the task of creating the graphics: he nipped across to one of the terraced streets behind Yorkshire Television's studios, selected a door and clicked his camera. The door formed the backcloth to the titles, and its simplicity, together with the accompanying theme tune, provided one of the most memorable images in the sitcom genre.

LIGHTING-UP TIME

The sets on *Rising Damp* were very effective, yet designer Colin Pigott is the first to point out that he wouldn't have achieved such results without the skill of lighting director Peter Hardman, someone he worked with for over ten years at Yorkshire Television.

Rising Damp was the first sitcom Peter ever lit and it posed a challenge. 'I had to ensure I got over to the viewers the dinginess of the place, which wasn't easy because in those days you had to light to certain engineering requirements, making it difficult to get the atmosphere of this grubby rental accommodation. Back then it was usual to make situation comedies very bright and flat. *Rising Damp* was one of the first where it wasn't right to do that: we needed more contrast and depth,' explains Peter, who went on to light most of Eric Chappell's sitcoms for Yorkshire, including *Duty Free*.

The lack of space within the sets posed another challenge for Peter, who clocked up nearly thirty years with Yorkshire after moving from ABC in 1968. 'It meant the lighting was coming into the set from a fairly steep angle, which was tricky for the cameramen. It was difficult getting light to the artists' eyes, which, of course, is essential, but you had to do it without destroying the depth and feel of the sets.'

Rising Damp is one of the best shows Peter – who now works freelance – has worked on, and people still talk to him about it. 'Recently, after finishing another programme in the studio, I went for a drink in the bar, where people were talking about *Rising Damp*. I still think it's brilliant, so well written.' But if he was working on it today, Peter admits he'd do his job differently. 'I would make it darker for a start: I still think it's too bright. With modern cameras you have so much more flexibility, whereas the ones I used back in the seventies weren't particularly brilliant and you were restricted. I would ensure more light came through the windows, while the set would be much darker; I would want a much softer feel to the picture, too. In lighting terms, soft light is much kinder to faces, more natural and produces softer shadows.'

LIGHTS, CAMERA ... ACTION!

Working closely with the lighting director were the cameramen. During the four series of *Rising Damp*, several cameramen worked on the show, including Colin Philpott, who has worked in the industry for forty years. Just as it did for the lighting director, the size of the sets presented a test for the cameramen. 'The sets were meant to be compact because that was the sort of house they were living in. There was no room for artists to move, which is probably why they weren't called upon to do much movement in terms of dramatic pieces; the problem tended to be that you had four or five pieces of furniture fighting for the same floor space.'

The sitcom was recorded using several cameras, which required coordination within the production team. As Colin explains, an orthodox practice was followed when problems occurred: 'If the issue revolved around cameras, it tended to be sorted out by the operator himself, but occasionally some reference to the director might be required, especially if a couple of cameras were fighting for the same space or shots.

'There were other problems which involved shots not working because of what the artists are doing; that suddenly moves from being a technical person's problem and becomes an artist-related problem – something the director has to sort out. It might be the cameraman wants the artist to move: if you work well with the artist you can sometimes organize that yourself and it's acceptable to both the artist and the director. But you don't suddenly start saying things like: "Can you delay that move from A to B by a line or two?" because that's altering the artist's movement, which is something they've already rehearsed.'

Colin would travel to London on the Wednesday, together with a sound technician, to watch a rehearsal. If he could foresee any difficulties it gave him a chance to sort everything out with the director in time for the recording. 'As the series progressed we reached the point where I would have read the following week's script as well, meaning I could discuss any points with the designer and be working a little ahead of schedule.'

Some of the sets were built on a rostrum. Although this proved effective in terms of creating the illusion of the characters living in a real multi-storey house, it restricted the camera team in some ways. 'The attic room was at least a foot off the ground, whereas Miss Jones's room was on the level. The difficulty with a set on a rostrum is that the flexibility as to where the camera crew can go to take some shots is inhibited because obviously he can't lift his camera up or penetrate into the set to take a shot.'

Although such sets meant the height a camera could reach was sacrificed, it was compensated by how low the equipment was able to go, enabling the cameramen to create an effect by filming from low angles. 'Lifting the sets was to help generate the feeling of being high up: if you were looking out through the attic door you got the impression of the staircase going down from the room; somebody could walk round the corner and go down the stairs, or that's what it looked like.'

One aspect of Eric Chappell's writing which appealed to Colin was the long scenes. 'Often on sitcoms, especially now, you might only get twenty or thirty seconds on a particular scene, rather like a soap opera, before you cut to another location. That interrupted the flow, in my view, but Eric always wrote long scenes. You might even find that one part of the episode was based around just two or three scenes. The artists seemed to prefer long scenes because they were able to develop the characters, and good sitcoms are all about the people.'

DRESSING UP

While Colin Pigott and his team were busy designing the sets, Brenda Fox set about establishing the dress style of the characters. As the Senior Costume Designer at Yorkshire Television (she retired from the industry in 1987), she was usually allocated shows regarded as atypical or which contained an experienced cast. As soon as she read the scripts she knew the sitcom had potential. 'They were extremely good and I had a feeling it was something which would capture the public's imagination,' Brenda says. 'When I worked for the BBC, I had the same feeling about *Monty Python*, not that I was the designer on it, but the girl that did was in my office, and you get a feeling about a show.'

When it comes to creating the image of a character, the costumes worn have to reflect their personality or style; being the first to work on the series, Brenda's job was crucial in setting the tone for the rest of the show. When it came to designing a wardrobe for Rigsby, she drew inspiration from the original stage play, *The Banana Box*. 'The character was called Rooksby in that, and it gave me an idea, because he was very much like a rook. He was rooted in his house and never seemed to go out,' says Brenda, whose first job after graduating from art college was with the BBC. Because she thought Rigsby spent most of his day padding about and prying on his lodgers, she gave him plimsolls to wear. 'They were quiet, which meant he could creep about and enter everyone's room without them being aware. He knew every creak in his own house, so he avoided every stair or floorboard that creaked.'

Brenda believes Rigsby could be viewed as a 'northern version of Alf Garnett', albeit 'softer' because he was still searching for romance.

There was one particular aspect of the character she felt was important to highlight in his dress. 'His sleaziness was crucial. The threadbare, sleeveless cardigan was picked up at a second-hand shop, and so were his trousers, while we made about six shirts for him.'

The tight schedule for producing a weekly episode meant Brenda, who worked on many top shows, including *Russ Abbot's Madhouse* and *Sez Les*, wasn't able to do any advance preparation; it wasn't until attending the read-through in London that she knew the requirements. 'After the first reading I would have a chat with the director, but then I was left alone to get on with the job because they knew what I could do.'

The technical limitations of the cameras back in the seventies required the costume designer to be careful when using certain colours. 'The cameras couldn't tolerate red, white, black and certain blues, so you had to consider that.' The dimly lit sets and drab colours, all vital in creating the general mood of the house, also posed challenges for Brenda and her team. 'With Don I tried giving him soft colours and small patterns which would fetch up his skin tone. And his character was smart and slightly arrogant, so he always dressed accordingly.'

'When it came to Miss Jones her clothes were fairly boring, but her style was often changing,' explains Brenda. And when Miss Jones was upset she would turn to the famous blue glasses, first seen in the pilot. 'The cameras couldn't tolerate plain lenses because the glass used to reflect the lights, so if they were made out of coloured glass it wasn't a problem. Frances always wore high-heeled shoes so that her character could clump about, look rather gawky and loom over Rigsby. Miss Jones was feminine but not really in control of her femininity.'

Of the four central characters, Alan was the easiest to sort out. 'He was very straightforward: he wore sweatshirts, which were new at the time, and jeans. He also had a suit and a tweed jacket which came from a shop called Take Six. I didn't have to do much shopping for him, but I remember one occasion we went out shopping together and he was mobbed by girls! For shoes he usually wore desert boots or tennis shoes.' Alan also started off the sitcom wearing a wig because he'd been filming *Porridge*; he didn't reveal his own hair until the episode 'Stage Struck'. 'The first wig was pretty dreadful and it was much better when he grew his own hair.'

Assisting Brenda on *Rising Damp* was Issy Berry, who is now Head of Costume at Yorkshire Television. One vivid memory she has of working on the show was being asked to dress the skeleton that hung around in Alan's room. 'I don't know who it was but someone wanted some clothes on it, so I rushed to the stock cupboard and returned with a bobble hat and scarf!' She took the rather unusual request in her stride. 'It's like that on entertainment programmes, you get asked to do some strange things.'

Just like set designers who often have to make wallpaper and carpets look old and grubby, Issy recalls having to scruff up Rigsby's clothes. 'To make his cardigan threadbare we would have made a small hole with scissors and then pulled the thread. We also used things like Vaseline and shoe polish to make things look greasy and dirty.' Even his trousers didn't go untouched. 'When you wear trousers for some time you end up with shiny patches, so we had to rub neutral polish into the fabric, which gave it a shine – it was very realistic. The trousers were quite old when we got them anyway, but it's surprising how something which looks old to the eye, seems quite good on camera.'

Chances are some refugee in a desperate part of the world is now wearing Rigsby's threadbare cardigan, if it survived the trip. The ragged item, which became the landlord's trademark, was until recently held in the stock cupboard at Yorkshire Television in Leeds. But a recent clear-out saw it end up in a charity box set up to help support some worthy cause. One item of his scanty wardrobe still residing at Yorkshire is the mucky-coloured dressing gown worn in episodes including 'The Permissive Society' and 'A Body Like Mine'.

She may have worked on plenty of shows since *Rising Damp*, but Issy, who worked for an opera company before joining Yorkshire, still has happy memories of her time on the sitcom. 'It was such fun and was one of the first shows I worked on. You couldn't help but laugh at what was going on, it was such a funny show.'

MAKING UP
Di Lofthouse (née Caplin) was the first make-up designer assigned to *Rising Damp*. She worked in the department for nearly twenty years before emigrating in 1989 to New Zealand, where she owns a vineyard with her husband. After attending the read-through in order to check there were no special requirements for that particular episode, Di and her team wouldn't see the cast again until the day of recording.

'The script had to be broken down as far as make-up and hairdress-ing requirements were concerned,' she explains. 'Then, during the read-through, the director would tell you if he wanted anything in particular for any of the characters. If anything was required, I would offer ideas.'

Di regards the role of make-up designer as being as much about PR as actual make-up techniques. 'You had to liaise with the actors, the director and Eric, the writer, to make sure everyone was happy with how you planned making up an artist; there's no point moving ahead if someone's unhappy. As far as the artist is concerned, you could well be the last person they see before going on the set. If they're not happy when they leave your chair, it could affect their performance.'

When it came to planning how she'd make up the artists for *Rising Damp*, Di had to visualize the characters Eric Chappell had created. 'I had to forget about what the actors actually looked like and try to imagine what the characters would be like; then you decide how to transform the actor into the character they're playing.'

The style of sitcom meant Di had to downgrade most of the characters. 'Rigsby was a sleazy, down-and-out type of character, whereas Leonard was a smart, dapper sort of man. Richard had to wear a wig because his hair wasn't long enough, because his character was a bit of a layabout with lank hair. And even with Miss Jones you had to make her look frumpy, whereas Frances isn't.'

STAGE MANAGEMENT

The stage manager is at the heart of the production team, a crucial component ensuring events run smoothly and to plan. This master coordinator is involved from day one, liaising with the set and costume designer, discussing requirements with the props buyer, passing script changes on to the PA (whose job is to update the scripts) and keeping his or her finger on the pulse as the day of recording draws nearer. Other duties include setting up and helping run the rehearsals, acting as prompt during rehearsals and assisting the director wherever necessary. When it comes to recording, the stage manager takes charge of prop and scene changes. In the early days, one stage manager was assigned to the show, but as the series progressed the workload became such that two people, like Olive Simpson and Terry Knowles, were employed.

One of the first tasks was to get the rehearsal room ready for the actors' arrival by using the set plan to mark up the floor, showing the exact size of the sets. This was not always an easy job, as Olive Simpson, who'd been an actress before working as a stage manager for twenty years, explains: 'Once I'd got a copy of the ground plan from the designer, which had all the sets marked out in scale, I marked them out in the rehearsal room, which, of course, was smaller than the studio. It was very complicated but quite fascinating, and the idea was to show the rooms with the correct spacing so that if an artist walked in the door and across to the table, everything matched what it would be in the studio. To achieve this I sometimes had to overlap rooms, using different-coloured tape to indicate where one room ended and the other started.'

Next, furniture had to be organized to replicate items to be used in the studio. 'Every single prop and piece of furniture used during rehearsals had to be found for the recording. During rehearsals decisions would be made where a particular item would go, so we'd move all the props around with the actions, making sure everything was in the agreed position back in the studio.'

Continuity could often cause problems and the stage manager had to be alert. 'If we stopped recording for some technical reason, we might have to return and reshoot a previous scene before the artist had done something, like move cups away from the kitchen sink or cut a piece out of an apple pie; if you went back to a shot before all that happened I had to have my prop man ready with replacements. Therefore you needed all these extra props just in case you did a retake.'

Although the lion's share of the stage manager's job was completed during the rehearsal process, there was still plenty to do in the studio, as Terry Knowles explains: 'If anything occurred during rehearsals involving props and sets, I would have to brief the props crew and the scene crew, ensuring what came into the studio was what the actors required.' Terry also had to ensure any trick props or visual effects were organized. In the final episode, 'Come On In, the Water's Lovely', he had to create the effect of steam. 'Rigsby was enjoying a curry with Miss Jones, but knowing the vapour coming off the curry wasn't going to register on the camera, I had to arrange for something to be put in the curry to make it steam and appear very hot,' says Terry, who retired from the industry in 1998. 'Sometimes if the food wasn't going to be eaten we'd include a substance used in the dry-cleaning process: it actually smoked but gave off a terrible acrid smell, so you couldn't get very close to it. We also used dry ice at times.'

PROPPING UP

A vital cog in the huge production wheel of television is the props buyer, who beavers away behind the scenes ensuring sets are perfectly equipped when it comes to recording. The principal buyer on *Rising Damp* was the late Gil Proctor, but occasionally other people helped out, like Rod Saul. 'We would spend very little time in the studio and would hardly ever see the stars of the show,' he says. The first time the props buyer became involved in the production was when the designer, Colin Pigott, passed him a shopping list of items required to help dress the set. It was then the buyer's job to obtain the items, either from stock or by purchasing them elsewhere. 'Often the designer actually comes round and checks the items himself: for example, if he wanted a settee and a couple of chairs, we'd take him to a place where he had a selection and he'd make the ultimate choice.'

Just like the set designer, one of the main challenges for the prop buyer on *Rising Damp* was getting items which looked dirty enough to qualify for inclusion inside Rigsby's squalor. 'We needed to keep certain items as dirty as possible, and we often used a company which specialized in such matters, but we always looked for items as run-down as possible.'

Although some things were obtained from second-hand shops, often Rod, who spent twenty-five years at Yorkshire Television, would go to a hire company. 'Time is against you because you get very little lead time in comedy, so it made sense to acquire as much as possible in one go.'

RECORDING

Thirty minutes before the cameras started rolling, the audience was let into the studios. Recording in front of a live audience is always a critical point among actors when it comes to assessing the overall value of the final production. Unlike the theatre, where actors are performing for the audience, television recordings are all about acting for the viewers at home, so for many thespians having people in the studio as well is a distraction. But as far as producer Ronnie Baxter is concerned, he doesn't think you could make a very good sitcom without an audience, and believes no one should have any qualms about recording in front of an audience if the show is good. 'Hearing people respond to wonderful lines is an unbeatable feeling; it creates a tempo, sometimes like an express train, which is valuable to the overall recording.'

RUNNING THE FLOOR

While the director sits up in the control box during the recording of the show, the floor manager takes charge of the studio floor, acting as the director's eyes and ears and providing a vital link between the box and the actors on stage. While the episode is recorded, the floor manager will be in constant touch with the director, relaying instructions, giving cues and ensuring everything runs smoothly throughout the evening.

Three floor managers worked on the sitcom: Mike Purcell, Pat Richards and Don Clayton. Don worked at Yorkshire Television for twenty-three years before retiring in 1991, by which time he'd moved on to directing and producing. Since then a lack of opportunities in directing has seen him return to the floor on occasion as a freelancer. Don points out the floor manager can have a marked effect on how the recording day proceeds: 'A bad floor manager can make bloody hard work for whoever is upstairs in the box.'

He remembers his time on *Rising Damp* as hard work. 'Comedy can be very tough, especially when you're dealing with some strong personalities. Len Rossiter was brilliant in the role but very intense, and not necessarily the funniest man in the world to work with. I'm a fairly outgoing sort of bloke and usually seen in the bar after the production has finished, but on two occasions I was working on the series I got straight in my car and drove home because I was absolutely wrung out. There was tension between the director and Len, which I have to say was generated by Len: it wasn't anything malicious on Len's part – it was just that he was such a perfectionist, and got into the role so much, that he didn't always appreciate the producer. Ronnie Baxter was meticulous in my opinion, a first class producer–director who paid great attention to detail.

'If I had to go and stop Len for any reason, even during rehearsals, he would be a little bit short because he couldn't understand why we were stopping. Of course we were stopping for something Ronnie wanted, which was always for the good of the production, although Len, in my view, occasionally lost sight of that. But he was absolutely brilliant in the part and I'm sure it was because he got so caught up in the whole thing.'

But Don enjoyed working with the cast. 'Len presented some wonderful performances; Richard Beckinsale was very laid-back and had quite a calming effect on the production, and Don Warrington was a good lad.'

Looking back at the episodes he worked on, Don is particularly fond of two: 'Clunk Click' and 'Stage Struck'. 'There wasn't a bad one in the whole series,' he says. 'Even now, I roar if I start thinking about some of the episodes. The studio was oblong-shaped and because of the smallness of the sets we were able to create a studio which resembled an ordinary theatre auditorium, which made for a better audience situation. When we recorded "Stage Struck" we had to put out an extra two rows of seats because it was oversubscribed, and I remember the scene where Hilary decides to play Miss Jones's part in a scene from his play to get his own back on Rigsby, who's been telling Alan that he's queer. The audience just took off, it was such a wonderful situation. Normally when we stopped for a scene or costume change the warm-up artist went on, but we didn't need him after that scene because the audience had laughed so much. It's very rare you find that sort of situation today – there just isn't the richness of comedy.'

5

CAST AND CREW

Vital to the success of any television programme are a cast and a production crew who pull together. Schedules are tight and pressures
intense, but the professionalism shown by all involved – both sides of
the camera – went a long way towards making *Rising Damp* an enduring
favourite among sitcoms.

LEONARD ROSSITER
(Rupert Rigsby)

Rupert Rigsby is one of the world's worst bigots, a man riddled with prejudices, who resents anyone showing the slightest interest in Miss Jones.
Along with a brother who now lives in Accrington, Rigsby endured a
poor childhood, he claims. You never knew when to believe him
because his stories of the past varied from one day to the next, usually
to suit a particular point he was trying to make. On one hand he says he
lived on bread and dripping, went to school in gumboots and always
had stubby pencils because his parents couldn't afford new ones, while
we later hear him boast he's related to one of the most powerful families in the country. His recollections of the war years are just as suspect,
especially when he brags about serving in the desert and in France,
where his efforts were rewarded with a war wound, which now prevents
him attending church because he can't get into the pews.

Rigsby regards himself as a respectable member of the local commu-
nity, even though he's been banned by the British Legion for poking a
stripper with a stick of celery and runs what is probably the dirtiest and
dingiest boarding house in town. But for all his social pretensions, he's
insecure and gullible: not only was he taken in by the crooked Seymour
and the fake policeman who came calling in 'The Prowler', but when Alan
tells him a jar contains millions of deadly micro-organisms, he panics.

In his trademark attire of threadbare cardigan and grey trousers which have seen better days, he sneaks around the house, bursting in on his tenants, never giving anyone a moment's peace.

One thing we can be sure about as far as Rigsby is concerned, is that he's tight-fisted. Not trusting banks or building societies, he keeps his money on the premises, hoping one day to retire to Bournemouth. His stinginess sees him turn down the chance of taking Brenda out for a slap-up meal, and cross the other side of the road whenever he spots someone selling lapel flags for charity, blaming his action on someone once sticking a pin in his chest. And as Alan reminds him, he also collects all the bits of soap and sticks them together instead of buying a new bar.

When it comes to love, the only women Rigsby has ever fancied are Greer Garson and Miss Jones. His wartime marriage was a sham, and he classes it as a military blunder on the scale of Anzio. He describes his wife, Veronica, as a 'big lump', telling Ruth that when he tried putting his arms around her it was like 'trying to grab hold of a detached barrage balloon'. He admits to getting married for his own security: Veronica's father thought Rigsby had been tampering with his daughter and threatened him with a shotgun. After a honeymoon in Blackpool, the marriage went downhill rapidly, and eventually the couple separated. In the final episode Rigsby's divorce comes through and he declares that the relief feels like the time he had his plaster taken off in hospital, because he regards his chain-smoking wife, now residing in Cleethorpes, as a 'dead weight'.

Never to win the love of Miss Jones, Rigsby leads a frustrated, lonely life with his cat. Ever since children at the British Legion set his beard alight while he played Santa, he's disliked kids and won't allow any in the house. Another rule cast in stone prevents Alan and Philip bringing girls back to their room. He describes the place as a 'respectable house', though his motives for such a rule probably stem from his own sexual frustrations at not being able to woo Miss Jones: if he can't enjoy a love life, he's certainly not going to allow anyone else the pleasure.

'With a false nose that isn't and a mouth like the grin on a Halloween pumpkin, his face by itself is a piece of theatre,' was how one journalist described Leonard Rossiter. The words paint an exaggerated picture of the man, but there is no doubt that his physical features were very distinctive, as was his inimitable style of acting. And it was these qualities which propelled the actor to the top of his profession and are sorely missed today – seventeen years after his untimely death.

Leonard was one of the industry's great talents. His strengths and abilities were amply demonstrated in *Rising Damp*. But although he enjoyed playing Rigsby, and went on to appear in four series, each time a new season was being discussed he always thought carefully before committing himself, mainly because he avoided being associated with long-running shows. In an interview in the 1970s, he explained: 'I was in *Z Cars* back in the early 1960s, and they asked me to become a regular in the series. But I turned it down because I felt then, as I still do, that to go on playing the same role year in and year out could become very boring. I am one of those people who derive much delight in doing different things.' When it came to considering further series of *Rising Damp*, Leonard explained that he had to satisfy himself that 'one, the writer feels quite happy to go on writing, confident that he can maintain the standard, and, two, that I would continue to work with some, if not all, the same people. I wouldn't want to start again with an entirely different team.'

Born in Liverpool in 1926, the son of John and Elizabeth Rossiter, Leonard was educated at the city's Collegiate Grammar School. He excelled in languages and wanted to become a teacher – ambitions that were tapped during his national service. Rising to the rank of sergeant, he taught illiterate soldiers to read and write while based in Germany with the Army Education Corps. After demob, Leonard, who by now spoke French and German fluently, saw his plans to study languages at Liverpool University thwarted because his father, a voluntary ambulanceman during the war, had been killed during an air raid in 1942. With his mother to support, Leonard discarded the idea of teaching and joined the Commercial Union Insurance Company in 1948, earning £210 a year as a clerk in the claims and accidents department.

It was during the six years he spent in insurance that Leonard experienced his first taste of acting. 'Len always told the story about the evening he was picking a girlfriend up from the local amateur dramatics company,' says his widow, actress Gillian Raine. 'He sat at the back of the hall and watched, but wasn't at all impressed. When she asked him what he thought of the performance, he told her he could do better. She suggested he tried, so he did – and that was how his acting career began.'

An insurance clerk by day and a novice thespian by night, Leonard became the first of the Rossiter family to tread the boards when he joined a local acting company. His brother, John, was a scientist, while his father had been a barber. 'But he was also a bookie at a time when gambling was still illegal,' explains Gillian. 'While customers had their haircut they could also lay bets because he ran a secret bookmakers. He got to know many of the variety actors working in the city, and even played golf with George Formby's father.'

Leonard's stage debut was in Terence Rattigan's *Flare Path*, with the Adastra Players. A local critic reported that he had an inclination to speak his lines too quickly – something he was wise enough never to change and which became one of the hallmarks of his fine acting style. His incredible pace of delivery was something Gillian noticed when they first worked together in *Semi-Detached* at Coventry's Belgrade Theatre in the autumn of 1963. 'I remember saying to myself: "Oh God, how are we going to get this across to the audience? No one will ever hear what he says because he talks too fast." But, of course, the audience did, and they found him just as funny as I did.'

It didn't take Gillian long to realize Leonard had a bright future as an actor. 'It's impossible to say someone is going to become successful, because there is always a certain amount of luck involved in this business. But it was obvious Len had great talent and, given the right opportunities, would do well as an actor.'

Leonard's amateur days were becoming increasingly busy as he began working with more than one amateur society at a time. It was clear he'd reached an important juncture in his life: if he wanted to further his acting career he had to turn professional, which meant ditching his job as an insurance clerk. At the age of twenty-seven, he did just that. Swapping the stability and security of a regular income for the jobbing actor's precarious lifestyle was an enormous step. But he never let the pressures associated with the decision affect him: as far as Leonard was concerned, acting was his future; it was also far more appealing than living out his life in the boredom of an insurance office.

His professional career began at Preston Rep, playing Bert Gay in *The Gay Dog*. Two other members of the cast were John Barron and Frederick Jaeger, both of whom worked with Leonard in the successful BBC sitcom *The Fall and Rise of Reginald Perrin*. 'Len was dedicated and a perfectionist even in those days,' says Frederick. 'He was so intense about his work, which meant he wasn't the most relaxed of people. But he was always word-perfect and one of the most professional actors I've

ever worked with. He expected everyone to work as hard as he did. You
had to keep up with him, otherwise you'd know it!'

After Leonard left Preston, spells followed at Wolverhampton and
Salisbury before he joined the Bristol Old Vic Company at the city's
Theatre Royal. He felt the two seasons spent at Bristol were crucial
because they established a solid base from which his career could bloom.

By the mid-1960s Leonard had experienced working in all strands
of the entertainment world. His film appearances included Whymper in
A Kind of Loving, Phillips in *This Sporting Life* and Shadrack in *Billy Liar*.
On the small screen he'd already appeared in numerous productions,
such as *The Avengers* and *Z Cars*, playing the derisive Detective Inspector
Bamber. Whatever medium he worked in during his career, the love for
his favoured medium, the theatre, never waned. As Gillian explains:
'Many people remember Leonard solely for his TV work, yet he did
more stage work than anything else. Between TV projects he always
returned to the theatre, and got slightly annoyed whenever he was
referred to as a small-screen actor.'

Interviewed in the 1970s, Leonard pointed out he liked to 'play the
field'. He said: 'I do about three plays a year as a rule; I like to do films
now and again – who doesn't? – and I like to vary my television roles.'

Gillian's memories of the days spent working with Leonard at
Coventry in *Semi-Detached* are all happy ones: 'I can remember we
laughed all the time. The play was well written and very funny, but being
a new production, we had the chance to shape it the way we felt best and
Leonard's influence was crucial to this process.'

Leonard's career progressed well. Although he was not offered the
lead when *Semi-Detached* moved to the West End, he was given the opportunity of taking the play to Broadway – though he probably wished he
hadn't. After two weeks of well-received previews the critics turned against
the show when it opened on Broadway. Within a week it had closed.

In 1969 Leonard's brilliant virtuoso performance as Hitler in
Brecht's *The Resistible Rise of Arturo Ui* made him a West End star. In the
audience one evening during the play's successful run was Richard
Briers, who was impressed by Leonard's performance and recalls: 'His
energy in the part was extraordinary. He was one of the great eccentric
actors and certainly a one-off.'

This energy was acknowledged by Vernon Lawrence, who worked
with Leonard on the final series of *Rising Damp*. 'He had a terrific

appetite for dialogue and used to gobble up page after page; much of the energy and drive in the show came from Len.'

Some people found Leonard tough to work with and Vernon admits he was always prepared to speak his mind. 'I had a great relationship with him and I admired him enormously, but if something was wrong he certainly took no trouble in coming forward and telling you. He could be quite ruthless but had every right to be because he was a genius. I'm not saying he was an unpleasant man – just that he knew what he wanted and what was right for the show. He wasn't a selfish man and didn't insist on having every other line or taking centre stage all the time. If he felt the script contained something gratuitous and we were running over, he was only too happy to have his own lines cut for the benefit of the show.'

His occasional excursions on to the big screen continued and his television career was just as busy, but it was not until 1974 and the advent of *Rising Damp*, followed quickly by *The Fall and Rise of Reginald Perrin*, that Leonard Rossiter became a household name. Other TV roles followed, but nothing seemed to live up to the high standards set by these two vintage comedies. However, he did attract a fresh audience with a series of successful Cinzano adverts with Joan Collins.

There is no doubting Leonard was a perfectionist. He worked incredibly hard to make the most of whatever he was working on and expected the same degree of dedication from fellow thespians. Occasionally people viewed him as difficult to work with. 'Len wouldn't go along with things that he wasn't happy with and had the confidence to say something about it rather than put up with it. Because of this frankness some people felt he was difficult,' says Gillian. 'What people sometimes forgot was that playing the lead in many of the productions meant he carried a great amount of responsibility on his shoulders. If something wasn't of the highest possible standard it would reflect badly on him.'

Away from the spotlight, Leonard was a private man who enjoyed a variety of sports and was a connoisseur of wine. 'He was always energetic,' Gillian remembers. 'If we went on holiday we had to go somewhere that had squash courts. He wasn't the sort of person to sit on a beach. If we did, it wouldn't be long before he was up running along the beach.'

Leonard's career and life came to a shocking end while he was appearing in Joe Orton's *Loot* at London's Lyric Theatre in 1984. Appearing with Leonard in the play, ironically about death, was actor David John. He will never forget that tragic evening. 'The day before he'd told me he wasn't feeling very well because he had chest pains and planned to see the doctor. The following evening I asked how he'd got on at the doctor's and he said: "Fine. He gave me a check over and I'm as fit as a fiddle." That was that and we continued with the play.

'I was sitting in my dressing room when a call went out reminding Len that his entrance was coming up. I couldn't believe it because he was never late for one of his scenes. Then when I heard over the Tannoy the actors on stage improvising because they had run out of lines after Len had missed his entrance, I knew something was terribly wrong.'

David rushed to Leonard's dressing room, pushed the door open and found him slumped in an armchair. 'The first thing I noticed was his grey complexion. Initially, I was so shocked I didn't know what to do, but within seconds other members of the cast arrived. Gemma Craven felt his pulse and said he was dead. I couldn't believe it and tried giving him the kiss of life and massaging his heart. I just couldn't imagine he was dead, but I was wrong. When the ambulancemen arrived I still thought there was a chance he would be OK, especially when they put an oxygen mask over his mouth. But when I saw two of the doctors who'd been in the audience shake their heads to each other as he was carried from the dressing room, I knew there was no chance. The rest of the evening was a blur as we finished the performance. The play continued for a further three months before it finally closed.'

Leonard had died of a disease of the heart muscles, a congenital defect that could have struck at any time. That evening the world lost one of its finest actors and his talents are still sadly missed.

FRANCES DE LA TOUR
(Ruth Jones)

An admin officer at the local university, Ruth Jones is a lonely woman whose spinster lifestyle often leads to bouts of depression and lack of self-confidence (she once belonged to the local badminton club but left because no one spoke to her). Unlucky in love, she has had a few relationships but each has ended in dismal failure. She is a frequent migraine sufferer, and with each bout her famous blue-tinted glasses make an appearance. Ruth was a wartime baby. Her mother is still alive, but her father met his death on Guy Fawkes' Night in the early 1970s. Suffering a heart attack, he collapsed in the street, but everyone kept stepping over him mistaking him for a Guy.

With a job going nowhere, a room with a view dominated by a gasometer and no admirer waiting to whisk her away, life is bleak for Miss Jones. Short of attention from the opposite sex, she gains a little solace from the lecherous Rigsby, who throws compliment after compliment in a non-stop drive to win her affections. He frequently tells her she's brought a touch of refinement and quality to the house, and that she possesses an 'hourglass figure', although she wishes she had 'a bit more sand'.

A member of the local Women's Guild, occasional actress – she once made a brief appearance (her character was strangled in the first scene) in an amateur production of Shakespeare – and one-time model for gloves, Miss Jones gets so desperate for love that she accepts Rigsby's proposal of marriage in the final episode, only to get cold feet and not turn up at the church. Not that it mattered, because Rigsby ended up going to the wrong venue anyway.

Although Ruth Jones's life didn't abound with men, we do get to hear of some of her failed romances during the sitcom's run. When she was younger she dated a policeman who always insisted on wearing his uniform. The trouble was, people always thought she was being arrested, so they had to swing their arms to prove they weren't handcuffed together. Her relationship with the bobby didn't last long.

Although we never hear of Miss Jones getting married, she came very close to it with a man she regarded as 'sensible and plausible'. But when he saw the wedding presents something snapped inside him and he fled. The last Miss Jones saw of him he was driving off in a hired minivan with his father clinging to the roof. To make matters worse, he swiped all the presents.

In 'Moonlight and Roses' Miss Jones strikes up a relationship with Desmond, the bespectacled librarian who flatters her with poetic chatup lines. She leaves her rented room to marry, but predictably everything falls apart before they walk down the aisle.

Eventually Miss Jones became so desperate to find a partner she turned to a matrimonial agency, but, as we learn in 'Pink Carnations', her luck didn't change. She was put in touch with a 'fun-loving extrovert with an urge to travel' and was impressed until she discovered he was serving time at Parkhurst. The next candidate was better, but didn't measure up to her expectations because he didn't even reach her shoulder. On their first date, she had to lift him off the bar stool. She tried her hardest, but the last straw came when she started developing a stoop.

Although she soon realizes her decision was a bit hasty and based on desperation rather than love, Miss Jones accepts Rigsby's proposal of marriage in the last episode, 'Come On In, the Water's Lovely'. But this goes wrong too. Perhaps for Miss Jones, life holds nothing more than surviving alone in a bedsit.

From the moment *Rising Damp* appeared on our screens, Frances de la Tour was keen to point out she didn't have a lot in common with Miss Jones. 'I may have had at one time, but certainly haven't now. I was brought up a little like her – she has middle-class values and these were instilled into me when I was young – but there the similarity ends. The only thing I can say about the character is that I was able to draw upon my own background experience in creating her.'

Although Frances enjoyed playing Miss Jones, and her face became instantly recognizable to millions because of it, she prefers working in the theatre, where the roots of her career lie. 'I liked *Rising Damp* because it opened up a new dimension to me, and it was a challenge. But even in television situation comedy one can draw profitably from one's theatre experience.'

Vernon Lawrence, who directed the final series of *Rising Damp*, enjoyed working with Frances. 'She's incredibly talented. In the series she played off Len with that wonderful coy, flattering demeanour. Of course, she's gone on to be hugely successful in many other demanding roles.'

Born in Bovingdon, Hertfordshire, Frances trained at the Drama Centre in London before establishing a busy career on stage and screen. Shortly after graduating she joined the Royal Shakespeare Company in Stratford, and during her six years there she turned her hand to many stage roles, such as Miss Hoyden in *The Relapse* and Belinda in *Man of Mode* at the Aldwych Theatre. Among her vast list of theatre credits are Helena in Peter Brook's production of *A Midsummer Night's Dream* in Stratford, New York and London, Tennessee Williams's *Small Craft Warnings*, in which she played Violet, a performance that won her the Play and Players' Award for Best Supporting Actress, *Duet for One* by Tom Kempinksi (Evening Standard Award and S.W.E.T. Award for Best Actress), *Moon for the Misbegotten* by Eugene O'Neill (Olivier Award for Best Actress), *St Joan* by Bernard Shaw, the title role in *Hamlet*, Miss Belzer in *When She Danced* (Olivier Award for Best Supporting Actress) and most recently Cleopatra in *Antony and Cleopatra* with Alan Bates.

On the small screen Frances has played various roles, including Maud Cole in *Flickers* in 1981, Emma Porlock in the 1996 mini-series *Cold Lazarus*, Rosemary in *Downwardly Mobile*, Shirley Silver in *Every Silver Lining*, Millie Renfrew in *Ellis Island*, Paddy Bysouth in *Stay Lucky*, Celia in *The Bounder* and the Honourable Tessa Blundle in an episode of *Heartbeat*. Frances has also appeared in a number of films, including the big-screen version of *Rising Damp*, for which she won the *Evening Standard*'s Best Actress Award.

Although her career has been built on much more than *Rising Damp*, repeats of the sitcom keep the image of Miss Jones firmly in one's mind. 'She was an interesting character to play,' admits Frances. 'We laughed a lot on set, but comedy is a serious business and Leonard took it particularly seriously, and rightly so. Comedy, which is so much down to timing, is exhausting work. But it was a happy time.'

RICHARD BECKINSALE
(Alan Moore)

Alan Moore is a medical student at the local university, although the thought of him eventually treating the sick and needy frightens Rigsby, who constantly reminds him about the time he examined Vienna's leg because of a limp, only to end up dislocating the cat's hip. He'll also never forget the time Alan went to the aid of a man in the basement and pronounced him dead. Three hours later the man was snoring.

The long-haired Alan (who always uses curlers at night) is a shy, inexperienced young man who returns home every weekend. Rigsby claims he's mollycoddled, especially as his mother blows on his hot potatoes for him. When he's back in bedsitland he likes to pretend he's a ladykiller, although when it comes to girls his lack of experience is clearly visible. Alan was a delicate child and still suffers from prickly heat and nosebleeds, but he has grown up to be a likeable, friendly sort of guy.

Richard Beckinsale's sudden death at the age of thirty-one was tragic. As well as robbing his family of a loving husband and father, it deprived the world of showbusiness of one of its finest talents, an actor whose shining career promised even greater things. With several hit shows under his belt, Richard was already sought-after, particularly by television.

Although he had a desire to expand his portfolio beyond the naïve but agreeable men he was usually asked to play, his performances in such roles were always top-notch, as writer Eric Chappell explains: 'He was a great actor and you never saw the cogs going round.' Richard's abilities afforded him seamless performances, so much so that Eric admits he was often guilty of taking his efforts for granted. 'It's only in retrospect, after watching the episodes again or talking about him, that you realize just how good he was. Because he made acting look easy you didn't rate him as highly as others.

'He was a very accomplished actor and if he was alive today he'd be playing all sorts of roles. He was surprisingly disarming with his talents: at times I felt he didn't have much ambition and limited himself, which wasn't the case but just the impression he gave at times. When you saw him do something else you realized he could do almost anything. I watched him in several stage plays and his performances were always impressive. Sadly, we didn't get to see and appreciate his full range.'

When interviewed in 1970 for a Yorkshire Television press release, Richard expressed his desire to move on to more mature roles. With *The Lovers* and *Rising Damp* both requiring him to portray impressionable young men, he said: 'I'm getting a bit old for this type of role. I want to move on and play older parts.' But he always made a success of his comedy roles, and didn't ever regret accepting parts like Alan in *Rising Damp*, Geoffrey in *The Lovers* and Lennie Godber in *Porridge*. 'I've always been selective, especially where comedy series are concerned. I have been lucky in that I accepted three offers in television comedy within a relatively short space of time which have become hits. But I have also turned down several offers which I feel pretty sure would not have been hits.'

Born in Nottingham in 1947, Richard left school at sixteen determined to become an actor. Before his dream came true, he worked as an upholsterer and a clerk in a pipes factory while studying English and art at night school. But when he was offered a place at RADA, he headed for London and a new career.

After graduating from drama school, Richard – whose daughters Kate and Samantha are both actresses – worked in rep, before more extensive theatre roles, such as Romeo in *Romeo and Juliet* at the Leeds Playhouse in 1971, came his way. Soon small parts on television were being offered, including a 1969 episode of *Coronation Street*, in which, as PC Wilcox, he had to arrest Ena Sharples.

Richard's big break came in 1970, playing Geoffrey, alongside Paula Wilcox, in Granada's sitcom *The Lovers*. Two series were transmitted and his performance as the young Mancunian bank clerk won him an award as Best TV Newcomer for 1971. The show became a big hit with viewers, and by the time *Porridge* and *Rising Damp* were running in the mid-1970s, Richard was a familiar face all over Britain. Other television credits included *Couples, Second House, Tales of Piccadilly, Elephant Eggs in a Rhubarb Tree, Give and Take, Truscott's Luck* and *Consequences.*

Although the success he achieved in sitcom brought security, Richard was always on the hunt for fresh challenges on screen and stage. In 1975 he was offered a straight role in the TV film *Last Summer,* while in the theatre he was seen in productions of Shakespeare as well as in various musicals and satires. In 1979 he had moved on to a new BBC sitcom, *Bloomers,* written by James Saunders, when he tragically suffered a heart attack. Rehearsals were due to begin on the sixth episode of the series when he collapsed suddenly at his home. The five episodes already recorded were later transmitted with the blessing of his widow, the actress Judy Loe.

DON WARRINGTON
(Philip Smith)

A student of town and country planning at the local university, Philip Smith secures a room at Rigsby's house courtesy of Miss Jones, who fancied him the first time she set eyes on him. Although she's never to get her man, Miss Jones, who described Philip as a 'real gentleman', is always prepared to help him if there's anything he needs.

Well-spoken with a refined, phlegmatic manner, Philip is not one of Rigsby's favourite people, especially when he boasts about being the son of an African chief and having ten wives. These claims are never substantiated in the TV series – unlike in the original play and subsequent film – and it's clear that he's pulling Rigsby's leg.

Self-confident and a hit with the girls – he claims he lost his virginity at fourteen – Philip strolls through life without a care in the world, another factor which irks his landlord.

Don Warrington will always be remembered for playing Philip in *Rising Damp,* an amazing achievement given that it was his first television job after graduating from drama school. Reflecting on how he set about portraying the suave, well-educated student, Don once said: 'It's not an easy role. The comedy situation is that of a black being more English than the

English themselves. But it's like walking a tightrope. If I were to go over the top it would be a caricature and therefore not funny.' He added: 'Philip must always be very real, very acceptable, if he's to be amusing.'

For an actor fresh from drama school, being a crucial member of a small sitcom cast is a golden opportunity to introduce yourself to the huge audiences that television attracts. But, as Don once explained to journalist Romany Bain, it was a very apprehensive young actor who stepped on to the *Rising Damp* set for the first time. 'It was the most nerve-racking time of my life at the beginning. My first television job, and I had very little experience of comedy.'

Don is quick to point out that Leonard Rossiter gave him valuable encouragement in the early days. 'He was very helpful to me. He could smell a laugh hidden away in quite an ordinary line. He used to take me aside and say: "Don't try so hard. Don't say it that way. Just try it like this." He was always right.'

Director Vernon Lawrence worked with Don on the fourth series of *Rising Damp* and prized the experience. 'He was a joy to work with and I was fortunate because when I joined the series he was given much more to do because Richard Beckinsale had left. Whereas he might have been a bit quiet in the previous series, he suddenly had to carry more of the script. I was watching an episode the other night and he carried the whole of the first half – he was the pivotal figure. It was hugely demanding and he rose to the challenge.'

In a vein running throughout the sitcom, the opinionated Rigsby often hit out at Philip with sarcastic, racist comments. But the show offended few people, partly because Philip always ended up with the upper hand, firmly in control of the situation, and made his landlord look a fool. In an interview with the *Sun* in 1975, Don said: 'Philip is far too sophisticated and well-educated to be made to look foolish.'

Born in Trinidad, the son of politician Basil Warrington, Don came to England when he was eight and lived in Newcastle upon Tyne. With a keen interest in the theatre since boyhood, he left school and worked as an assistant stage manager at the city's Playhouse Theatre, before training at the Drama Centre in London for three years.

Shortly after leaving the drama school in 1972, Don spent three months in the European production of *Hair*. In addition to his appearance in Eric Chappell's *The Banana Box*, he worked a season at Lincoln Rep, appearing in productions such as *A Taste of Honey, Erpingham Camp,*

Measure for Measure and *Dutchman.* His extensive theatre work has embraced spells with the National Theatre, in shows including *Dispatches, The Passion, The Mysteries* and *Three and Me,* and plays such as *The White Devil, Macbeth, Julius Caesar, Eldorado, A Midsummer Night's Dream, Resurrections* and *Ear, Nose and Throat.*

Among Don's other television credits are *Crown Court, Six Days of Justice, Carbon Copy, Club Havana,* Jomo Ibbon in *The XYY Man* in 1976, Johnson in *Fairly Secret Army,* Bold in a 1985 episode of *Juliet Bravo,* Commander Binks in *Red Dwarf,* Nigel Beaumont in three series of *C.A.T.S. Eyes* and Hari Ben Karim in *Arabian Nights.*

Although many people will always regard Don as a comedy actor because of his role in *Rising Damp,* he has gained experience in all strands of the profession, playing a multitude of roles. 'I never thought of myself as a funny man,' he admits. 'I shall always be proud to be connected with such a successful series, but I would also like to be thought of as a straight actor.'

Appearing in successful sitcoms, especially shows which survive the ravages of time to become classics, brings welcome exposure for any actor. But it can also prevent a career blossoming as he or she would like. Although Don has gone on to appear in many other stage and television shows, he did suffer typecasting for a while after playing Philip. He told the *TV Times*: 'The problem with being so heavily identified with a particular series is that no one wants you to do other things. That happened to me. For a long time I was typecast and, although I've struggled against it, I suppose to a certain extent it's still true.' But he was keen to point out that the cast all got on very well, often enjoying nights out together after recording in Leeds, and that 'making the series was a great time in my life'.

The Directors

IAN MACNAUGHTON
(Producer and director of pilot episode)
Glaswegian Ian MacNaughton abandoned his medical studies during his first year to join the Royal Marines in 1942, although his preference had been the Fleet Air Arm. He was placed in an officers' training squad at Deal, in Kent, where he was given a chance to act with the Globe Players, the marines' amateur group.

After demob in 1946, Ian spent a year in his father's engineering and outfitters' shop in Glasgow, but quickly realized it wasn't the life for him. Spotting an advertisement inviting applications to study at the Royal Academy of Dramatic Art in London, he tried his luck, with the full support of his family, and was accepted.

Once he had graduated from RADA in 1950, he joined the Citizens' Theatre, Glasgow, and spent the next eleven years acting on stage and screen. While appearing in a BBC drama series, *Silent Evidence*, he read an article in *The Times* that led to another change in direction, this time to behind the camera. BBC2's imminent arrival meant the Corporation needed more directors. Ian applied for the job and was recruited, although he continued acting for a while. When he eventually found it difficult juggling two jobs, he opted for directing, and worked on an episode of *Z Cars*, as well as *Doctor Finlay*, *The Troubleshooters*, *The Revenue Men* and *This Man Craig*.

But Ian is best known for his work on Spike Milligan's *Q* series and *Monty Python*. He now lives in Munich, where he's retired from television, although he'd return to work if the right project came along. Since leaving Britain, he has directed operas and musicals, and has worked in Germany, Israel, Yugoslavia, Norway and Austria.

RONNIE BAXTER

(Producer and director of nineteen episodes: all except pilot, 'All Our Yesterdays', 'Things That Go Bump in the Night' and fourth series)
Salford-born Ronnie Baxter completed national service as a photographer in the RAF, and on returning to life as a civilian pursued a career in TV. He joined ABC Television in 1966 as a cameraman, before attending a training course in directing. He qualified as a director and worked on *Candid Camera* and other shows until the ITA's reshuffle in 1968 took him to the newly formed Thames TV.

In 1974, Duncan Wood, ex-BBC and then Head of Light Entertainment at Yorkshire Television, contacted Ronnie and asked him to join the company to produce and direct *Rising Damp*. The rest of Ronnie's career as a producer and director was spent at Yorkshire, and although he's now semi-retired, he'll happily return to work if the right script comes along.

LEN LURCUCK
(Producer and director of two episodes: 'All Our Yesterdays' and 'Things That Go Bump in the Night')
Len was born in London and studied design at college before doing national service in the RAF. Returning to civvy street, he began his television career as a cameraman with Associated Rediffusion in the mid-1950s, before being invited to set up the camera department at Yorkshire Television on its inception in 1968.

A few years later he was given the opportunity to transfer to the Light Entertainment Department and try his hand at directing, with one of his first projects being *Hello Cheeky*, a series originating on radio back in 1973 with Tim Brooke-Taylor, John Junkin and Barry Cryer. Len, the only staff director in the department at that point, worked on a few pilots before helping to set up the *Rising Damp* pilot; he was later given the chance to produce and direct two episodes.

Len continued working for Yorkshire, including spells on *Emmerdale Farm* and eight years on education programmes, before he retired in 1989. He turned freelance for a while but is now fully retired from the business. Nowadays much of his time is taken up with charity work, including regular stints in Ethiopia, where he teaches the indigenous people how to make television programmes.

VERNON LAWRENCE
(Producer and director of the fourth series)
Born in London in 1940, Vernon Lawrence was educated at Dulwich College and Kelham College. He gained, but didn't pursue, a place at King's College, London, to read theology.

After a range of jobs, including being a novitiate monk in a Church of England order, a Butlin's Redcoat for a season and an orderly in a mental hospital, he joined BBC Radio in 1959 as a studio manager, working in both overseas and domestic broadcasting. He eventually moved into light entertainment and worked on many popular shows, such as *Round the Horne*, *The Goon Show*, *The Navy Lark* and *Take It From Here*.

By the age of twenty-four Vernon had been promoted to radio producer in the newly established Popular Music Department, producing shows like *The Ted Heath Band* and *The Vera Lynn Show*. He moved to BBC Television in 1965 and within three years was producing and directing shows for both the comedy and variety departments, among them *Lulu*,

The Production Team

(Except where otherwise stated, the team members performed their respective jobs throughout *Rising Damp*.)

SCRIPT: Eric Chappell.

PRODUCER: Ian MacNaughton (Pilot); Ronnie Baxter (Series 1, except episode 4; Series 2, except episode 7; Christmas Special); Len Lurcuck (Series 1, episode 4, and Series 2, episode 7); Vernon Lawrence (Series 4).

PRODUCTION ASSISTANT: Mary Byrne (Pilot; Series 1); Celia Sherman-Fisher (Series 2); Evelyn Hirschstein (Christmas Special; Series 3); Ellie Kyle (Series 4).

STAGE MANAGERS: Terry Knowles and Olive Simpson.

MUSIC: Dennis Wilson.

COSTUMES: Brenda Fox (Pilot; Series 1–3 and Series 4, except episode 6); June Cashman (Series 4, episode 6).

MAKE-UP: Di Caplin (Pilot; Series 1, except episode 6) Jane Clifton (Series 1, episode 6); Viv Locklin (Series 2; Christmas Special); Pam Fox, Pearl Rashbash and Pat Reid (Series 3); Judy Binns (Series 4).

CAMERAMEN: Mike Boyle, Colin Philpott, Arthur Tipper and Peter Lord (Pilot; Series 1); Gerry Lord, Mike Boyle, Colin Philpott (Series 2; Christmas Special); Arthur Tipper, Gerry Lord, Colin Philpott (Series 3); Paul Thompson, Colin Philpott, Gerry Lord, Dave Ramsey (Series 4).

SOUND: Ron Parker and Ian Hughes (Pilot; Series 1); Dave Whiteley, Chris Warner and Ian Hughes (Series 2; Christmas Special); Ian Hughes and Chris Warner (Series 3); Glyn Edwards, Ian Hughes, Dave Whiteley and Chris Warner (Series 4).

Jazz at Ronnie Scott's, Top of the Pops, Cilla and *Beyond a Joke*. In 1972 he spent a year with the Arts Features Department and directed *Omnibus* and many editions of *Full House*.

At the invitation of Sir Paul Fox, he moved to Yorkshire Television in 1974 as Executive Producer, Light Entertainment, and went on to produce and direct hit shows like *Rising Damp, Only When I Laugh, Song by Song, Duty Free* and *The Harry Secombe Series*. He was appointed Controller of Entertainment in 1985 and instigated such successful programmes as *Home to Roost, The New Statesman, A Bit of a Do, The Darling Buds of May* and *A Touch of Frost*.

Vernon left Yorkshire Television in 1993 to join the ITV Network Centre as Controller of Network Drama and Entertainment. Among the many shows he commissioned were *Cracker, Band of Gold, Kavanagh QC, Cadfael, The Knock, The Governor, Outside Edge, Frank Stubbs* and *Moll Flanders*.

In 1995 Vernon set up a new company, MAI Productions (now known as United Productions), to coordinate all Network offers for both Anglia, Meridian and subsequently HTV. As Managing Director, he was responsible for increasing programme output and selling to both ITV and other major broadcasters. In 1997 he became chairman of the company, but has now retired from the business.

LIGHTING: Peter Hardman and Peter Squires (Pilot; Series 1–2 and Series 3, except episode 6); John Watt (Series 3, episode 6); Peter Hardman (Series 4, except episodes 5 and 6); Bob Gray (Series 4, episodes 5 and 6).

VISION MIXER: Kay Harrington, John Cooper and Chris Foley (Pilot; Series 1); Kay Harrington and Chris Foley (Series 2); Jackie O'Gorman (Christmas Special); Sue James, Kay Harrington and Jackie O'Gorman (Series 3); Sue James, Chris Foley and Kay Harrington (Series 4).

DESIGNER: Colin Pigott (all episodes except Series 4, episodes 3, 4, 5 and 6); Colin Pigott and Peter Caldwell (Series 4, episode 3); Peter Caldwell (Series 4, episodes 4, 5 and 6).

6

OTHER TENANTS

Anyone staying at Rigsby's boarding house must have been a glutton for punishment, exposing themselves to such harsh, torrid conditions; and if you weren't heavily dosed up on anti-depressant when you arrived, you certainly would be if you were fortunate enough to escape. Although Rigsby occasionally mentioned past tenants while conversing with his regular lodgers (namely Alan, Philip and Ruth), the only other people daft enough to rent a room quickly headed off to pastures new. The loud-mouthed wrestler Spooner and the shapely model Brenda gritted their teeth and stayed a while, but others, like the depressed Mr Gray, only paid a fleeting visit to the Rigsby household – not that anyone can blame them.

MRS BRENT's stay at the house is short-lived. In 'That's My Boy', which opened the third series, she's given a room by Alan while Rigsby is off sunning himself in Spain, although he ends up spending most of his holiday in the police cells. But when the grisly landlord returns early from the Med, Mrs Brent and her young baby, David, are forced to find new accommodation quickly. Before her departure her husband, Jim, who works as a merchant sailor on cross-Channel ferries, arrives on leave.

Wolverhampton-born actress ANN BEACH played Mrs Brent, a role that involved a baby. Several shots of the smiling infant are shown during the episode, but when it comes to cast members lifting it from its cot, a doll was used. 'I was a bit nervous about using the lifelike doll because if the camera caught this corpse of a baby it would give the game away. They used dolls much more in the seventies, but I always got a little worried,' says Ann, who started out as a singer.

'I moved to Cardiff when I was about nine, and because I had a singing voice I got swept up into lots of events, including broadcasts with the BBC Wales Orchestra, but my first job was in a BBC production of the opera *Hansel and Gretel*.' Ann wanted to make a career in opera, but won a scholarship to RADA instead; although her career has involved many musicals, she has remained an actress ever since.

On graduating from drama school she went straight into the West End, playing the lead in Emlyn Williams's *Beth*. She later joined the famous Joan Littlewood's company at Stratford East and worked at the Royal Court, before television parts started being offered, beginning with live broadcasts in Manchester. 'They were pretty hairy things to do,' smiles Ann. 'I remember once my character was supposed to shoot somebody and the gun got stuck in my pocket! I ended up pointing my pocket and shouting: "Bang!" I had no choice but to get on with it.'

The Unseen Tenants

From time to time Rigsby would mention a past tenant, and most of them seemed oddballs who would have been better off under medical care than residing at the lodging house. In 'The Prowler' we learn that the previous occupant of Alan and Philip's room drilled a hole in the floorboards and peered through to watch Miss Jones undress in the room below. And in 'Stand Up and Be Counted' Rigsby tells us about the tenant who used to jump every time he opened the door, to the point where Rigsby believed he must have been in trouble with the police. In 'The Good Samaritans', the previous tenant in Mr Gray's room took to the roof in his underpants. He was self-employed, up to his neck in debt and blamed the Labour government for his depression. Rigsby had to call the vicar, who saved his life: not by talking him down but by breaking his fall when the man jumped.

There was the guy who supposedly suffered blackouts: on one occasion he came round to find himself clutching a black chiffon nightie outside the local Marks & Spencer. And then there was the Indian who fancied himself as something of a cordon-bleu cook and used to arrive back at the house with twenty-four friends piled into a single taxi. He left owing a month's rent.

Ann's small-screen credits include *The Rag Trade, Steptoe and Son, Nanny, Only When I Laugh, The Winslow Boy, Cranford, The Government Inspector, Blodwen, Brookside, Land of Hope and Gloria, The Bill* and *The Lifeboat*, but her biggest success was playing the chatterbox neighbour Sonia Barratt in four series of John Chapman's successful sitcom *Fresh Fields*.

On the big screen Ann has appeared in a handful of films, such as *On the Fiddle, City of the Dead* and *Under Milk Wood*. Nowadays she concentrates mainly on radio and audio projects, including recording most of the *Famous Five* audio books for Chivers Press.

The cravat-wearing HILARY is a second-rate thespian who spends more time 'resting' than treading the boards. His unremarkable acting career has nosedived since a sprained ankle saw him miss out on a part in *Oh! Calcutta!* His biggest role to date involved running around squeezing grapes wearing a stag's head in the orgy scene of *I, Claudius*. Nowadays all his agent has to offer is tacky revues involving nude scenes.

In 'Stage Struck', Hilary recruits Alan and Ruth to act out his play, a 'psychological drama'. His habit of calling his landlord 'ducky', and his liking of Alan's 'cascading' hair, makes Rigsby question the limp-wristed Hilary's sexuality.

London-born and RADA-trained PETER BOWLES became a professional actor at eighteen, and after graduating from drama school spent a year at the Old Vic, before moving into repertory theatre. One of the highlights of his early career was appearing in *Happy Haven* at the Bristol Old Vic. His vast body of stage work includes appearances in *Absent Friends, Dirty Linen* and *Born in the Gardens*.

On TV, he became popular with audiences as Neville Lytton in *Lytton's Diary*, Howard Booth in *The Bounder*, Archie Glover in *Only When I Laugh*, Featherstone in *Rumpole of the Bailey* and the highly successful Richard De Vere in *To the Manor Born*. Among his other credits are *The Avengers, The Saint, The Prisoner, Space 1999, The Survivors, Churchill's People, I, Claudius, Executive Stress* and *Perfect Scoundrels*. Peter also made several films, including *Blow Up, The Charge of the Light Brigade, Eyewitness* and *Laughter in the Dark*.

Appearing in *Rising Damp* meant meeting up with Rossiter again, whom he'd worked with at the Bristol Old Vic back in his rep days. One moment he'll never forget is a terrible row the two actors had. 'We were a double act in a panto called *Hooray for Daisy!* recalls Peter. 'It got a bit tricky because my comedy timing was different from his; when it came to choosing a style which was right for our roles we couldn't agree and ended up having a tremendous argument. Even so, I enjoyed working with Len and we developed a great respect for each other.'

The experience of working with Rossiter put Peter in good stead when they met on the set of *Rising Damp*. 'When I arrived at the studios I sensed immediately that everyone seemed nervous of him. They kept warning me not to upset him because he was very particular. I'd always got on well with Len and by now we were old friends. When filming began I started making suggestions about how scenes could be improved. Everybody seemed to duck for cover but, as I expected, he listened and we tried out my ideas. I could never understand why everyone was so nervous, because if you put forward a good idea which was worth trying, he would never dismiss it.

'Len was a remarkable actor with a unique style. I remember his spring-footedness more than anything: it was as if he had springs in his shoes. His stylistic approach was very powerful and was something he was unaware of until later in his career, when he began exploiting it. He was a great actor.'

Peter remains busy in the profession, particularly in the theatre.

In 'Suddenly at Home' OSBORNE is constantly mocked by Rigsby because of his sickly disposition. There is no doubting the lanky Ossie, who is of a rare blood group, is a hypochondriac. He spends so much time at the local hospital, Rigsby claims he has his own chair and was consulted over the colour scheme when the surgery was decorated. He consumes so many pills he rattles as he climbs the stairs from his basement flat. Renting the worst room in the house, Osborne is pitied by Miss Jones, who cooks for him every day.

ROGER BRIERLEY, a native of Stockport, played the lanky, hypochondriac Osborne, who featured in just the one episode. Appearing in the sitcom was a memorable time for Roger, and not just because he enjoyed the role. 'My son was born the evening I had to catch the train to Leeds to record the episode. Just as I was leaving, my wife announced she needed to get to the hospital, and I replied: "I've got to go to *Rising Damp*." But it was my son who was being born, so the hospital took priority. His birth occurred at 7.20pm, by which time there weren't any trains between London and Leeds.' Needing help, Roger phoned a friend who worked as a lighting director for Yorkshire Television. 'I caught a milk train to York and he met me at 2.30 in the morning; I had a couple of hours' sleep at his place in Harrogate before reaching the studio, so it was a very memorable job!'

After the recording, Leonard Rossiter shared Roger's good news with the audience. In the episode Rigsby, believing the neurotic Osborne is going into hospital to have a vasectomy, tells him he's a young man who'll want to have children one day, and he won't be able to if he has his 'firing-pin removed'. Leonard stepped forward and said: "I'd just like to tell you that Osborne doesn't need to worry about having lead in his pencil because Roger Brierley, the actor who plays him, has just had a son who was born last night."' The announcement received a huge round of applause from the audience. 'So my son was born and within twenty-four hours he was getting a tremendous ovation at Yorkshire Television.'

Roger will never forget his appearance in *Rising Damp* because it's wrapped up in his life for obvious reasons; but he also enjoyed playing the character. 'It was a very good episode. The script was great and the character wonderful to play – I just wish I had that much hair now!'

The seventies was a busy decade for Roger as far as sitcoms were concerned. 'I worked on almost every show, including a couple that Ronnie Baxter produced, like *In Loving Memory*.' He recalls: 'Ronnie was great to work for. He knew exactly what camera angle he wanted, and I don't think there is anyone better in the business.'

Roger, who has made over 200 TV appearances, appeared in amateur dramatics from the age of fourteen. However, after leaving school he didn't pursue an acting career immediately, but qualified as a chartered accountant. It wasn't until he was completing national service that he decided to make acting his future. Returning to civvy street, he joined Bristol's Old Vic Theatre School, a decision which didn't please his father, also an accountant. 'He hardly ever spoke to me on the matter, he was so appalled. But he gradually got used to it, especially when people came up to him in the street and said they'd seen me on television.'

Roger then had four years of repertory work, before venturing to London with the aim of breaking into television. He achieved his goal appearing as Julian in an episode of *The Likely Lads*. Other TV parts quickly followed, including appearances in *Doctor Who*, *Telford's Change*, *The Politician's Wife*, *Jeeves and Wooster* and *Pennies from Heaven*. Roger has also been seen in a handful of films, among them *Superman II* and *Young Sherlock Holmes*.

Whatever work he completes in the future, Roger will always have a soft spot for his appearance in *Rising Damp*, a show he still enjoys watching. 'Success on television is down to the writing, and Eric Chappell hit on a great idea. But it would never have worked without somebody extraordinary in the lead role, and Len was one of those actors who wasn't afraid to play unloved characters. Rigsby was awful, but you end up having sympathy for him when you've no right if you consider it logically: you want to throttle him but somehow end up liking him. It was a remarkable performance from Len Rossiter, who was a wonderful actor,' says Roger, who nowadays finds himself cast in roles of authority. 'Most of the characters are judges, doctors or vicars – all authority figures; but I suppose that's partly because I'm tall, wear half-rimmed specs and often dress in a suit.'

A mature theological student, GWYN WILLIAMS studies at the local college and is usually seen clutching his well-thumbed Bible. A devotee of the Primitive Church of First Day Witness, Welshman Gwyn leads a strict lifestyle, intolerant of gambling, drinking, smoking, bawdiness and fornication. It's through the donations of fellow followers that he is able to study. The opinionated, overbearing religious freak possesses a magisterial manner which influences Rigsby for a while, but he eventually packs his bags when Miss Jones gets a little too close for comfort.

JOHN CLIVE was seen as two characters in the sitcom: the pipe-smoking Samaritan who rushes to the aid of manic-depressive Mr Gray in 'The Good Samaritans', and the Bible-bashing tenant Gwyn Williams in 'Fire and Brimstone'.

John was a busy character actor when asked to play the Samaritan, his favoured part. 'I'd worked with Ronnie Baxter before, so he knew my work, and I loved playing the Samaritan. It was a delight to appear with Frances de la Tour, whose subtle performance complemented whatever you did. I thought the episode worked rather well, especially as Eric's writing was so good: the scripts were extremely funny and proof of that is the fact that it's stood the test of time; here we are twenty-five years later and it's still going strong.'

Whereas John was pleased with the performance in 'The Good Samaritans', he wasn't too keen on the booming theological student. 'I was somewhat forced to play him very high up the scale, but what I wanted to do, since Rigsby is forceful and loud, is play it much more quietly; unfortunately I wasn't allowed to do that. In the end my character got louder and louder and it almost became a shouting match between Rigsby and Gwyn, and I didn't feel that was the best way to play it.'

John, who's a Londoner, began acting in rep as a child, appearing in plays like *The Winslow Boy* and *Life with Father*. His break arrived while working as a pageboy at a theatre. Hearing about auditions for a children's show, he submitted his name and was taken on as a boy singer, as well as assisting the resident comic in sketches.

His face has since become familiar from more than 100 film and television performances. On the big screen he appeared as a car manager in *The Italian Job*, *Carry On Abroad*, *A Clockwork Orange*, *Great Expectations* and *Revenge of the Pink Panther*. On television his credits include *The Sweeney*, *Wear a Very Big Hat*, *How Green Was My Valley*, *The Government Inspector*, *Casualty*, *Perils of Pendragon* and the lead (Professor Sommerby) in the children's series *Robert's Robots*. He has also appeared with most of the great British comedy performers, including Dick Emery, Tommy Cooper, John Cleese and Peter Sellers.

Today most of John's time is dedicated to writing screenplays and novels – he has written six to date – although he still acts if the right part comes along.

AMBROSE runs a stall in the local market in 'Under the Influence', earning much-needed cash as a mystic, although Rigsby has doubted his ability ever since a woman's hair fell out after he sold her a suspect tonic to cure lethargy. Rigsby also scoffs at Ambrose's claims of being a Romany, saying the only time he's been in a caravan was for a week's holiday in Cleethorpes. Although Ambrose's skills at hypnotism are unpredictable, he does succeed in hypnotizing Rigsby for a brief period.

Bristolian PETER JEFFREY, who was born in 1929, played Ambrose in the character's sole appearance, in the penultimate episode. Educated at Harrow and Pembroke College, Oxford, he graduated from RADA and worked in repertory theatres up and down the country – including a season at Bristol Old Vic with Rossiter – before becoming a familiar face on the small screen. His TV credits include playing Philip

II of Spain in BBC's 1971 classic *Elizabeth R*, Mr Peabody in *Jewel in the Crown*, Colonel Bernwood in *Lipstick on Your Collar*, *The Planemakers*, *Triangle*, *Porridge*, *Lovejoy*, *The Detectives* and *One by One*.

His notable stage work included being a member of the Royal Shakespeare Company for more than thirty years, while on the big screen he was seen in several pictures, such as *Becket* (1964), *The Odessa File* (1974), *Midnight Express* (1978) and *Britannia Hospital* (1982). Peter died in 2000.

The buxom MARILYN, who appears in 'Fawcett's Python', is regarded as a 'loose woman' by Miss Jones when she discovers the voluptuous entertainer spends the evening working with Charlie, her pet snake. An erotic snake dancer by trade, the brassy blonde has Alan and Rigsby falling over themselves to help. But with Miss Jones's continuing dislike for the woman, coupled with the fact that Rigsby believes she's a prostitute, it seems Marilyn will have to go. However, she's saved from packing her bags when Rigsby discovers she's only a dancer, although as Miss Jones points out, she still takes her clothes off.

Playing Marilyn was an enjoyable time for ANDONIA KATSAROS. 'When my agent called and said they wanted me to play an erotic snake dancer I couldn't help but laugh, but I jumped at the chance of appearing in the show because I thought Leonard was wonderful. Working with him in rehearsals was very interesting because he was like an electric typewriter: you never knew when the scene ended because he would just go on – he was so full of energy.'

Guesting on a sitcom can mean an artist isn't automatically welcomed into the fold by the regulars, but this wasn't the case when playing Marilyn. 'Sometimes you feel a little uncomfortable, but *Rising Damp* was great, and Leonard Rossiter always made me feel part of the group,' says Andonia.

Playing an erotic dancer meant Andonia had to work with a rubber snake, but trying to make it look realistic was no easy feat. 'It took a bit of work and Leonard probably did a better job than me, but we had little time to practise because we didn't get it for the first couple of rehearsals.'

Andonia was twenty-four when she moved to England from New South Wales, Australia, in 1969. By then she was an established actress back home, and had appeared in the film *Age of Consent*, with James Mason and Helen Mirren. When she expressed an interest in moving to

England, Mason introduced her to his agent, and it wasn't long before she was appearing in lunchtime theatre. Television work soon followed, beginning with the role of a Swedish masseuse in *Please, Sir!* Other credits include *Romany Jones, Porridge* and a regular part as a neighbour in LWT's drama *Helen – A Woman of Today* in 1973. Andonia also played Norma in the 1974 pilot of the BBC sitcom *Mr Big*, Melvina Walker in the TV mini-series *Shoulder to Shoulder*, as well as appearing in *Two's Company* and films including *Loot* and *Time After Time*.

Since 1978 Andonia has been living in America. Although she's made the occasional screen appearance, including a 1997 episode of NBC's sitcom *Suddenly Susan*, most of her time is spent touring her one-woman show. She's also a qualified pilot and taught flying for a couple of years.

In 'Hello Young Lovers' ROBIN rents a room to share a night of passion with his lover, Lorna, but they're mistaken for newly-weds by Rigsby and Miss Jones. Thinking Robin is inexperienced in matters of love, the inadequately qualified Rigsby tries offering some fatherly advice, but when he discovers they're simply using his room for a little hanky-panky, he gets Miss Jones to contact Lorna's father.

London-born ALUN LEWIS played Robin and within a few months of playing the character he'd worked with Leonard Rossiter a further two times, in BBC2's *Fearless Frank* and the short film *Le Pétomane*.

Alun was eighteen when he joined RADA in the early 1970s. After graduating he spent two years working at Lincoln's Theatre Royal, three at the Young Vic in London and a year at the Manchester Library Theatre. Spells at various reps followed before he made his television debut in a BBC *Play for Today*. He has appeared in many shows over the years, including *Van Der Valk, Rumpole of the Bailey, Charley's Aunt, Crown Court, Angels, The Professionals, Minder* and *Beryl's Lot*, but he's probably best remembered for playing Daryl in six series of *Birds of a Feather* and Vic Windsor in *Emmerdale*.

At the moment Alun is touring the country with *The Woolpackers*, a music band.

After he arrives at short notice, it's not long before SEYMOUR, the biggest fraudster in town, has the gullible Rigsby under his spell in 'A Perfect Gentleman'. Thinking the world of his new tenant, even though he can't get any rent from him, Rigsby is blinded by Seymour's financial claptrap. With as much business acumen as Vienna, Seymour – who hogs the bathroom – bluffs his way through life, preying on people like Rigsby. Although Rigsby thinks he's a financial wizard, especially when he advises him to invest in oil production in the Pennines, Seymour is nothing more than a dissembler: he's not a public-school-educated financial consultant who plays golf with the mayor and lives at The Manor with his wife, but a pickpocketing cad who's out to con Rigsby and his tenants.

HENRY McGEE believes one of the reasons he was offered the role of Seymour was because Eric Chappell felt he was adept at playing sinister characters. 'It's probably the most interesting part I've ever had on television; the episode was shown just the other week and people are still coming up to me saying: "You're Seymour!" It's very unusual for people to remember the name of a character who only appeared once, but then Eric has a great knack of hitting on wonderful names that fit the characters.'

It wasn't the first time Henry, who was born in London, had appeared in a piece written by Chappell, having played a leading role in *The Spanish Dancers*, the writer's first piece of work for television, dating from 1971. 'I'd never heard of Eric before but his script had magic in it – I thought it was wonderful,' says Henry, who noticed the same magical ingredients when he received the *Rising Damp* script.

Henry had little difficulty deciding how to play Seymour. 'It was simple because it was so clear from the writing what sort of character he was – it came alive off the page. Working on *Rising Damp* was a very happy experience; it was the only time I worked with Leonard but he was very inspiring because he had enormous energy. It was great fun.

'I've watched some repeats recently and have become even more impressed with the show because you appreciate the timelessness of it; the wonderful witticisms flow so smoothly, although one knew Eric put blood, sweat and tears into their creation; but the finished product is as light as air. It's a programme you could always show, partly because Eric never put in any topical gags.

'Eric's scripts were always so good; often when you receive a script you end up disappointed, but that was never the case with Eric's. He sent me one for an episode of *The Squirrels*. I was working in Windsor at the time and waited until after the matinée, then sat by the river and read it. I always remember it because it sent tingles up my spine – it was absolutely wonderful.'

Henry turned to acting after completing national service. 'My mother's family was connected to the theatre, which put me off joining the profession for a while. It's such a ludicrous business to go into because most people either give it up or starve to death, but eventually I decided acting was the only thing I had any natural aptitude for, so decided to give it a go.'

Henry is glad he followed his mother's example and joined the acting industry. After training for two years at the Italia Conti Stage School in London as a mature student he worked in numerous reps, including three years at Northampton. He then spent two years Down Under, playing the lead in a stage production of *For Better, For Worse*. After Henry returned to Britain, more rep work was followed by his TV debut in *Uncle Harry* for Associated Rediffusion.

His big break on the small screen came in 1965, when he played Mr Pugh, a clerk at the Labour Exchange, alongside Charlie Drake in *The Worker*. He went on to work with Max Wall, Frankie Howerd, Dick Emery, Reg Varney and Benny Hill, an association lasting twenty-three years. Henry hasn't worked on television for some years and for the last decade has concentrated on stage work, particularly Ray Cooney farces.

He's also made the occasional appearance in films, including *Sailor Beware* in 1956, *The Italian Job*, *Digby*, *Holiday on the Buses*, *Carry On Emmannuelle* and *Revenge of the Pink Panther*.

The loud-mouthed SPOONER is a wrestler whose professional nick-name, 'The Animal', befits the aggressive lodger who annoys everyone with his blaring radio and raucous singing. Spooner, who served as a Red Devil before entering the ring, is an inimical character who only has time for himself and his pet goldfish. Although he's seen in just two episodes ('Night Out' and 'All Our Yesterdays'), we learn in 'The Prowler' that he's away wrestling in Wolverhampton.

DEREK NEWARK was born in Great Yarmouth in 1933 and entered the industry late after enjoying a varied career. On leaving school he joined the merchant navy, where he stayed for three years before becoming a soldier. After serving with the Coldstream Guards he spent time in Singapore during the Malayan emergency. Before leaving military life behind after four years, he ran a radio show in Singapore playing country and western records, which gave him his first taste of the enter-tainment world. On returning to England he knew where his future lay and enrolled at RADA.

As soon as he graduated he worked in rep for many years before tel-evision and film work came his way. Early credits included *Z Cars, Out of This World*, playing a mess sergeant in *Redcap*, a reporter in *Front Page Story, The Baron, Man in a Suitcase, The Avengers, The Saint, Callan, The Champions, Department S, Jason King, Budgie, New Scotland Yard, Doctor Who, Coronation Street*, the 1965 movie *The Hill*, with Sean Connery, and, four years later, *Where Eagles Dare*.

He continued working in the theatre and the high point of his career came in the early 1980s when he was invited to join the National Theatre. He remained there for over a decade – an experience he relished because it gave him the opportunity to play a diverse range of characters, includ-ing Bottom in *A Midsummer Night's Dream*. Later small-screen appearances include Councillor Jack Winterbottom in *Juliet Bravo* and Corman in *Dempsey and Makepeace*. Derek died in 1998 of a heart attack, having become increasingly sick for several years.

For a while BRENDA replaces Miss Jones as the focal point of Rigsby's desires – and Alan's – after she is brought into the house by Alan in 'Moonlight and Roses'. (She also appears in 'The Last of the Big Spenders' and 'Things That Go Bump in the Night', as well the Christmas Special, 'For the Man Who Has Everything', which rounded off the second series.) Knowing Miss Jones was leaving to tie the knot with her librarian lover, Desmond, Alan was hoping the busty Brenda would take the room. Miss Jones's departure causes Rigsby heartache, but any pain is short-lived as soon as he casts his eyes over Brenda's vital statistics.

The outspoken, hippyish, curly-haired brunette, who works as an artists' model and poses for photographic classes, fled her previous accommodation because the landlord tried forcing his attentions on her, an experience which makes her wary as soon as the leering Rigsby arrives on the scene.

Brenda was played by GAY ROSE. Born in Canada, Gay, more often known as Gabrielle, trained at the Bristol Old Vic Theatre School for three years and spent a further six years working in Britain before the offer of a job back in her homeland was too good to refuse. Her deci-sion, at the age of six, to pursue a career in the entertainment world came as no surprise since Gabrielle's grandfather (L. Arthur Rose) was a playwright and producer who wrote *Me and My Girl* with Douglas Furber, which was later turned into a musical comedy by Noel Gay.

After graduating from drama school at twenty-one, Gabrielle, who's now forty-seven, completed a season at the Old Vic Theatre in Bristol, before the offer of small parts in several films came her way (including one with Leonard Rossiter) and the role of Brenda. 'At the time I was so self-conscious, but basically I was there to wiggle around and let the others get the laughs, which was all right with me,' she says, smiling. 'I was nervous because the cast, being so good, were a little intimidating. I'd only done a bit of TV so I was an inexperienced young girl, working alongside these hotshot actors. The night before recording I didn't get much sleep. But when I look back on the job it was fun; it wasn't a huge job but a nice break, and I got plenty of work from it.'

The job that persuaded Gabrielle to return to Canada in 1978 was Eliza in *Pygmalion* on stage in Edmonton, but film and TV work, including a role in the first season of *The X Files*, has been the mainstay of her career in recent years.

Gabrielle has recently given birth to her second child, and lives with her partner in Vancouver, but still misses Britain at times. 'I really enjoyed living in England, it was such a cultural centre. Until I got pregnant we were planning to spend a few months in England and France, but we couldn't make it. But I intend returning for a while sometime in the future.'

In 'The Good Samaritans' the dishevelled MR GRAY arrives late at night, claiming to have sunk to uncharted depths in fetching up in a place like Rigsby's. His gloom-laden face and deep depression have been caused by a woman who took him for every penny he owned, wrecking his marriage and business in the process. Rigsby discusses the plight of Mr Gray with the other tenants and ends up surmising that the downcast stranger – who has booked his room for just one night – is planning suicide.

DAVID SWIFT relished the role. 'I think a manic-depressive in comedy is always fun to play. People who know nothing else about my career always seem to have watched that episode of *Rising Damp*.'

Apart from the brilliance of Leonard Rossiter and the rest of the cast, David, a Liverpudlian, lauds the writing talents of Eric Chappell. 'It was pretty clear through the writing how the character should be played. With comedy you take a particular characteristic of the personality and exaggerate it, but you've got to choose the right one.' Although he acknowledges Mr Gray's circumstances were in many ways tragic, David feels the scriptwriter's skill in exaggerating his problems just far enough turned the situation into a scene which was esoterically funny.

'To work with Leonard was such a privilege because he was a genius. He knew what he wanted, and for someone so exceptionally talented he was surprisingly restrained. I've worked with other star actors who can take over, dominate and tell you exactly what to do. Leonard wasn't like that. He knew what he wanted to get from something but wasn't over-bearing, and was a delight to work with.'

Admitting he enjoys playing characters teetering on the edge, David adds that he likes watching the series even now. 'It's comedy for all time, it's wonderful. There's so much interaction between those extraordinary characters; it could almost have been recorded on a blank set because it would still have been hysterically funny. It was television at its very best.'

David – whose brother is actor Clive Swift of *Keeping Up Appearances* – qualified as a lawyer and worked as a businessman before turning to acting at the age of thirty. His first job was as an ASM at Oxford Playhouse, after which he spent four years in reps all over the country, including Salisbury, Leicester and Manchester.

Along with stints at the Royal Shakespeare Company and in the West End, television work arrived in the shape of educational pro-grammes for schools; but over the years he has appeared in *Going Straight*, *The Day of the Triffids*, *Bergerac*, *Within These Walls*, *Bloomers*, *War and Peace* and *Drop the Dead Donkey*. He's also worked in several films, such as *Jack the Ripper*, *The Next Man*, *No Sex Please, We're British*, *Travels with My Aunt* and *The Day of the Jackal*.

David has now retired from acting. 'I know it's immodest to say so, but it's not through lack of work; I just feel there are other things I want to do, like write, and I want to take things a little easier. I still get offers, and I'm not saying I won't act again, but I'm not actively seeking work.'

LORNA, who makes her sole appearance in 'Hello Young Lovers', is a student studying for a degree who rents a room briefly with her lover, Robin, and is mistaken for his wife by Rigsby.

DEBORAH WATLING enjoyed playing Lorna because she was a fan of the sitcom. 'I adored Leonard Rossiter, Richard Beckinsale and Frances de la Tour, so you can imagine my delight and excitement when I was offered the part. We rehearsed in a scout hut in Chiswick, and I have to admit I was slightly nervous and, of course, in awe. But there was no need because everyone was super, especially Leonard, who was a marvellous actor. It was like walking into a family, I was made to feel welcome from the beginning.'

Born into a showbiz family – her father was veteran actor Jack Watling and her sister Dilys Watling – Deborah made her acting debut at the age of ten, appearing as Sally Brady in an episode of the TV series *The Invisible Man*, before playing George Cole's niece in *Life of Bliss*. 'No one was surprised when I decided to become an actress; I knew instinctively it was what I wanted to do.'

Deborah went on to appear alongside her father in *Dr Who*, as Victoria Waterfield, and in the BBC's sixties soap *The Newcomers*. Other TV credits include *Arthur of the Britons*, *Out of the Unknown*, *Alice* and *Danger UXB*.

On stage she made her London debut in *A Bequest to the Nation*, followed by numerous other productions, including *Not In Front Of the Parents* and *The Wizard of Oz*. Deborah's big-screen roles started back in 1973 with *That'll Be the Day*, playing Sandra, a teenager who flirts with David Essex. Hard on the heels of this role was *Take Me High*, with Cliff Richard, in which she played a restaurateur.

Nowadays Deborah is mostly seen in the theatre, but she enjoys working in all mediums. 'I love it all,' she enthuses. 'But it's difficult because not a lot of good parts are written for women of my age, so you take what you can. I'm not old enough to play a granny yet, but I'm keeping going, which is good.'

7

A–Z OF OTHER FACES

In addition to the main cast and the actors who played Rigsby's less familiar tenants, thirty-three other performers were seen in the sitcom, all of whom appear below.

ELIZABETH ADARE
Role: Lucy
Episode: 'For the Man Who Has Everything'
In *The Banana Box*, the stage play that led to *Rising Damp*, the role of Lucy was part of the main cast. Elizabeth played the character during the pre-West End tour and at the Apollo Theatre in London. However, for the TV series, Lucy was relegated to just one appearance, as Philip's girlfriend, and Elizabeth took the part.

Elizabeth's other TV roles include playing Maggie in *Father Dear Father* in 1968, Carry in the second series of Thames TV's sitcom *The Setbacks* and six series of the company's sci-fi series *The Tomorrow People* in the 1970s. Elizabeth has also worked on a few films, including the 1970 picture *A Nightingale Sang in Berkeley Square*, in which she played a barrister.

ROY BARRACLOUGH
Role: Barman
Episode: 'Pink Carnations'
Roy qualified as a draughtsman and worked in an engineering factory for eight years. His spare time was spent acting with local amateur groups, but then he decided to quit his job and enter the world of entertainment full-time. He became entertainments manager at a holiday camp on the Isle of Wight, before joining Huddersfield Rep. He worked at various theatres around the country before making his TV debut in

the soap *Castlehaven*. During this period he met Les Dawson and their successful screen partnership was formed.

Although he's appeared in a handful of films, and has worked on radio and in the theatre, Roy is best known for his TV credits, which included *Nearest and Dearest, Love Thy Neighbour, Sez Les, Peak Practice, Mother's Ruin* and *Coronation Street*, playing Alec Gilroy.

NORMAN BIRD
Role: Vicar
Episode: 'Things That Go Bump in the Night'
Born in 1924, Norman entered the film industry in 1953, and made his TV debut three years later. On the small screen he has appeared in a host of shows, including *Ever Decreasing Circles, Worzel Gummidge, To Serve Them All My Days, Yes Minister, Lytton's Diary, The Practice, Second Thoughts* and *Boon*. His film career embraces appearances in over fifty titles, such as *An Inspector Calls, The League of Gentlemen, The Angry Silence, The Secret Partner, Man in the Moon, Victim, Whistle Down the Wind, The Punch and Judy Man* and *The Virgin and the Gypsy*.

JAMES BREE
Role: Peppery Man
Episode: 'Clunk Click'
James, who trained at the Central School of Speech and Drama, played the 'Peppery Man' in this episode from the third season, following Rigsby back to the house at the start of the show, angry about his standard of driving. Although James is still credited on the titles, the scene was cut when the show ran over its allotted time.

Spanning three decades, James's television work includes *The Prisoner, Doctor Who* and *The Avengers* in the sixties; *Upstairs, Downstairs, The Persuaders, The Sweeney, The Professionals, The Duchess of Duke Street* and *I, Claudius* in the seventies; and more recent appearances as a coroner in *The Return of Sherlock Holmes*, Colonel Grace in *The Jewel in the Crown, Executive Stress* and Mr Lambda in an episode of *Anna Lee* in 1993.

He has appeared in several films, including *Just My Luck* in 1957, *Never Let Go* in 1960 and the James Bond movie *On Her Majesty's Secret Service* in 1969.

RONNIE BRODY

Role: Charlie

Episode: 'The Last of the Big Spenders'

The son of music-hall artistes Bourne and Lester, Ronnie joined the merchant navy at fifteen, before serving with the RAF in North Africa during the Second World War. After demob he spent several years in variety and rep, but by the 1950s his career was dominated by film and television. Over the years he became one of the nation's most recognizable comedy character actors. Ronnie worked with many top comedians in shows like *Dave Allen at Large*, *The Dick Emery Show*, *Bless this House*, *Are You Being Served?*, *Home James*, *The Lenny Henry Show* and *The 19th Hole*. He has also been seen in films such as *Help!*, *A Funny Thing Happened on the Way to the Forum* and *Superman III*, as well as playing the little man in *Carry On Don't Lose Your Head* and Henry in *Carry On Loving*.

Although Ronnie concentrated on comedy, he appeared occasionally in TV drama. He died of a heart attack in 1991, aged seventy-two.

AVIS BUNNAGE

Role: Veronica

Episode: 'Great Expectations'

Playing the role of Rigsby's dreadful ex-wife was the respected character actress Avis Bunnage. Lead roles may have eluded Avis, but she made a good living playing a host of parts on screen and stage, usually down-to-earth working-class characters. However, her adaptability meant she felt equally at home playing classical roles.

While her father was a dentist, her mother was a variety performer, and after working as a telephonist and nursery teacher for some time, Avis joined the Chorlton repertory theatre in Manchester, making her professional stage debut in a 1947 production of *The Brontës*. In 1952 she joined Joan Littlewood's Theatre Workshop, an association that lasted more than twenty years and involved performances in the West End, France, America and South Africa. Her last stage performance was in the 1984 production, *The Way of the World*.

Avis's film career included roles in *Saturday Night and Sunday Morning*, *The Loneliness of the Long-Distance Runner*, *The L-Shaped Room*, *Rotten to the Core*, *The Wrong Box*, *The Spoils of War*, *Gandhi*, *No Surrender*, *The Whisperers* and *The Krays*, in which she played the grandmother. Her first TV appearance, meanwhile, was in the 1959 series *Probation Officer*. Other work in the medium included an eight-week stint in *Coronation Street*, *In Loving Memory*, *The Mayor of Casterbridge*, *Yesterday's Dreams* and *Inspector Morse*.

Avis died in 1990, aged sixty-seven.

JUDY BUXTON

Role: Caroline Armitage
Episodes: 'Clunk Click', 'The Cocktail Hour'
Judy's dream was to become an actress and as a girl she attended weekend drama classes. Having completed her A-levels, she joined the Rose Bruford College of Speech and Drama. After graduating she earnt her Equity card working as an acting ASM at Chesterfield Rep. A period of several years on the stage was followed by her television debut, playing a daughter in a 1972 episode of *Dixon of Dock Green*. Other TV work included a regular role in *General Hospital* as student nurse Katie Shaw, Ruth Carpenter in *On the Up*, *Get Some In!*, *The Mike and Bernie Show*, *A Woman's Place*, *Angels*, *Blake's 7*, *Masterspy* and Deborah Wyler in *Lovejoy*. Her last television appearance was in BBC2's *Close Relations*.

Since her appearances in *Rising Damp*, Judy's career has focused on the stage, particularly classical theatre, and includes three years with the Royal Shakespeare Company. However, recently she has returned to comedy, appearing in several Ray Cooney farces. Her West End credits include *A Murder is Announced*, *The School for Scandal* and *The Ghost Train*.

GEORGE A. COOPER

Role: Mr Cooper
Episode: 'The Permissive Society'
George, who's seventy-six and semi-retired, worked as a draughtsman in the concrete industry before turning to acting. After demob he joined an amateur company in Leeds before finally chancing his luck professionally at the age of twenty-three.

He made his debut at Kidderminster with Joan Littlewood's famous Theatre Workshop in the play *The Gentle People*. He toured with Littlewood's company before breaking into television in a BBC production of *Othello*. George's face has become well known on the screen, and among his numerous TV credits are *Z Cars*, *Mind Your Language*, *Grange Hill*, *Casualty*, *Billy Liar* and *Some Mothers Do 'Ave 'Em*.

He has appeared in over forty films, including *The Passing Stranger*, *Sailor Beware*, *Fortune is a Woman*, *Follow That Horse*, *Tom Jones*, *Nightmare*,

Smashing Time, On Her Majesty's Secret Service, Bless This House and *The Black Windmill.*

DAVID DAKER

Role: Mr Brent
Episode: 'That's My Boy'
David is a busy character actor who's been seen in many television shows over the years, including playing the temporary landlord Gordon Lewis in *Coronation Street* between 1981 and 1985. Other credits include *The Bill, Dalziel and Pascoe, The Midsomer Murders, Dangerfield, Casualty, The Vets*, Ben Campbell in the series *Crown Prosecutor*, Harry Crawford in seven series of *Boon, Moonfleet* and the first series of *Give Us a Break*, playing the pub manager Ron.

In addition to pursuing a busy stage career that includes many West End appearances, David has acted in films such as *Britannia Hospital, Time Bandits, Charlie Muffin, The Voyage, Aces High* and *The Black Windmill.*

ROBERT DORNING

Role: Father
Episode: 'Hello Young Lovers'
Robert trained as a ballet dancer, but before the Second World War turned to musical comedy. Following demob from the RAF, he resumed his career in musical comedies and increasingly moved into acting.

He worked for three years with Arthur Lowe in Granada's *Pardon the Expression* (they had previously worked together in *Coronation Street*), playing Walter Hunt. A well-known face on TV, he also spent four years in *Bootsie and Snudge* (1960–64) and appeared in series like *Bergerac.*

Robert made over twenty-five films, including *They Came By Night, Man Accused* and *The Black Windmill.* He also played the Prime Minister in *Carry On Emmannuelle.*

Robert's career had encompassed all facets of the entertainment world by the time of his death in 1989.

LIZ EDMISTON

Role: Maureen
Episode: 'Charisma'
Liz appeared in a single episode as Maureen, a girlfriend of Alan's, who's never seen without her racing bike. As well as *Rising Damp*, Liz has

appeared in numerous shows on stage and screen, including the 1973 film *Fourteen*, playing Sylvia, and various television programmes: an episode of *Never the Twain* in 1988, Alma Todd in the 1999 mini-series *Forgotten*, 1973's *The Wild Little Bunch* and 1977's *Holding On* for LWT, in which she played a washer girl.

JONATHAN ELSOM
Role: Douglas
Episode: 'Fawcett's Python'
New Zealand-born Jonathan, who now lives in Australia, clocked up forty years as a professional actor in Britain. He first came to Britain in 1959 thanks to a bursary from the New Zealand government which allowed him to study at LAMDA for two years.

After graduating he learnt his trade in rep, beginning with a summer season in Southwold, Suffolk. Eighteen months at Dundee was followed by work at Salisbury, Glasgow, Exeter, Canterbury, Windsor, Leatherhead, Hornchurch and numerous other companies around the country. His theatre career later extended to numerous West End productions, major tours and seasons at Chichester.

Jonathan made his TV debut in a BBC play in 1964, and has since become a well-known character actor in shows like *To the Manor Born*, *Minder*, *Bergerac*, *Regan*, *Lloyd George*, *Ladykillers*, *Danger UXB*, *Troubleshooters*, *Z Cars*, *The Baron*, *Across the Lake* and over 100 episodes of *Crown Court*. He also appeared as Ackroyd in a 1967 episode of *The Avengers*, and the following year popped up in *The Saint* as Andrew Carter.

His work in films has seen him appear in 1967's *Smashing Time*, 1979's *The Great Riviera Bank Robbery* as a magistrate, *Rough Cut*, *Ping Pong* and 1986's *Mesmerized* as a public prosecutor.

Jonathan also gained a Diploma of Fine Arts as a sculptor and has exhibited sculpture and paintings in London galleries. Examples of his work are in permanent collections in the UK, Canada, New Zealand and Australia. He also ran a theatre in New Zealand for a while.

DEREK FRANCIS
Role: Mr French
Episode: 'Clunk Click'
Derek built up an impressive list of theatre, television and film credits during a long career in showbusiness. On television he appeared in

programmes including *Ghost Squad, Jango, Undermind, Doctor Who* and *Man in a Suitcase* during the sixties, *Jason King, The Sweeney, Whoops Baghdad!, Nicholas Nickleby, Oh Father* and *The Professionals* in the seventies and an episode of *Keep It in the Family* in 1980, playing the Non-Mechanical Man.

On the big screen he was seen in over forty films, such as *The Criminal, Ring of Spies, The Hijackers, Press for Time, Scrooge, Man of Violence* and six *Carry On*s, playing Sir Edmund Burke in *Doctor*, a farmer in *Camping*, Bishop in *Loving*, a farmer in *Henry*, Arthur in *Matron* and Brother Martin in *Abroad*.

Derek died in 1984, aged sixty.

GRETCHEN FRANKLIN
Role: Aunt Maud
Episode: 'Great Expectations'
Gretchen was born into a theatrical family: her father was a comedian who formed a double act with her mother. She worked in a shop after leaving convent school, before entering showbiz as a chorus girl in a Bournemouth pantomime. Over the years she has forged a successful career for herself, working in all mediums, most notably television. Her small-screen credits include playing Elsie Ramsey in the pilot of *Till Death Us Do Part, Crossroads, The Ken Dodd Show, Crackerjack, George and Mildred, Churchill's People, Some Mothers Do 'Ave 'Em, Hazell, The Sweeney, General Hospital, The Harry Worth Show, In Loving Memory* and, more recently, Ethel Skinner in *EastEnders*.

HELEN FRASER
Roles: Gwen and Bride
Episodes: 'For the Man Who Has Everything', 'Pink Carnations'
Helen Fraser's love of the theatre came from her mother, who'd always dreamed of a showbiz career, and at the age of nine Helen attended a theatrical boarding school. She made her stage debut at fifteen in panto, in *Babes in the Wood* at the Hulme Hippodrome.

After studying at RADA she spent two years at the Manchester Library Theatre, before she started gaining experience on both the big and the small screen. Her busy television career has included roles in shows such as 1997's *The Uninvited*, playing a nurse, a neighbour in *The Patricia Neal Story*, the popular seventies sitcom *Doctor in Charge*, an episode of *One Foot in the Grave* as Dr Snellgrove, *Charlie's Place*, Gloria in

Father's Doing Fine and *Here I Come Whoever I Am.*

Helen's film credits include playing Barbara in *Billy Liar*, Mary Ream in *The Uncle*, Bridget in *Repulsion* and Lulu in *The Birthday Party*.

FRANK GATLIFF
Role: The Manager
Episode: 'Night Out'
Australian-born Frank, who died in 1990, at the age of sixty-two, was a character actor whose career kept him busy on stage and screen. As a regular on television during the sixties and seventies, he made appearances in *The Avengers, Out of This World, Department S, The Persuaders, Doctor Who, Robin's Nest* and *Blake's 7.* One of his last small-screen roles was playing a magistrate in an episode of David Nobbs's sitcom *Fairly Secret Army.*

On the big screen, he played a radio officer in the 1959 picture *On the Beach*, Major Palmer in *A Prize of Arms*, Bluejay in *The Ipcress File*, Dr Wilson in *The Projected Man* and many other roles.

ROBERT GILLESPIE
Role: The Gasman
Episode: 'The Last of the Big Spenders'
Robert was born in Lille, in France, and spent his early years in Nantes, until his parents moved to Manchester. He eventually began performing as a semi-professional at the city's Library Theatre, before joining RADA. After graduating he worked at the Old Vic in London until he was offered the role of Matthew in the TV production of *Jesus of Nazareth.*

Although Robert is normally cast in comedy roles, often as a policeman, with credits including five series of *Keep It in the Family, The Fall and Rise of Reginald Perrin, Robin's Nest, Butterflies, George and Mildred* and *Dad's Army,* he has also appeared in numerous dramas, such as *Maigret, Crane, New Scotland Yard, The Sweeney, Van Der Valk, The Professionals* and *Secret Army.*

Robert, who also writes and directs, has made several films, and frequent stage appearances, including two years with the Royal Shakespeare Company.

DIANA KING
Role: Mrs Armitage
Episode: 'The Cocktail Hour'
Diana, whose career was spent mainly in the theatre, always wanted to be

an actress and attended the Fay Compton School of Dramatic Art. During the Second World War she performed in various reps, including Peterborough and Buxton, and continued developing her stage career after the war. Later she also became busy on TV, appearing in many sitcoms, such as *Dad's Army*, *Marriage Lines* (as Prunella Scales's mother), *Are You Being Served?* (Captain Peacock's wife) and *You're Only Young Twice*.

Her sporadic film appearances began with *Spellbound* in 1941 and included *The Man in Grey*, *My Teenage Daughter*, *The Man Who Wouldn't Talk*, *A Farewell to Arms*, with Rock Hudson, and *They Came from Beyond Space*.

Diana died in 1986, aged sixty-seven.

IAN LAVENDER
Role: Mr Platt
Episode: 'Stand Up and Be Counted'
The son of a policeman, Ian had thought about being a detective but dropped the idea when he realized he would have to train as a policeman first. He turned his attention to acting and on leaving school headed for drama school at Bristol's Old Vic. As soon as he graduated, he completed a season in rep at the Marlowe Theatre, Canterbury.

Ian made his television debut in a 1968 TV play titled *Flowers at My Feet*, and during the same year appeared as Frank Pike in *Dad's Army*, the role for which he'll always be remembered. Since the classic sitcom finished in 1977, Ian has been heard on the radio and seen occasionally on the small screen, but he's been in most demand on the stage, appearing regularly in pantomime and theatre productions around the country. He has also appeared in a few films, including *Carry On Behind*.

LARRY MARTYN
Role: Fred
Episode: 'For the Man Who Has Everything'
Larry served with the parachute regiment during the Second World War and entered showbusiness in the 1950s, working in variety as a singer-comedian until the age of twenty-two. His early small-screen career was dominated by drama up to the 1970s, when he started being cast in light entertainment. His TV appearances include *Are You Being Served?*, *Dad's Army*, *The Dick Emery Show*, *Up Pompeii!*, *Mike Yarwood in Persons*, *Spring and Autumn*, *Never the Twain* and *The Bill*. He also made several films, such as *Up the Junction*, *The Great St Trinian's Train Robbery*, *Carry On At*

Your Convenience and *Carry On Behind*, playing an electrician. Larry died in 1994.

DAPHNE OXENFORD
Role: Radio Announcer
Episode: 'That's My Boy'
Daphne, the voice of BBC radio's children's programme *Listen With Mother* from 1950 to 1971, started her working life as an actress. But she'd made her West End debut much earlier, appearing in two Christmas plays while still at school. After graduating from drama school, she joined a theatre club before working in the West End and touring with musicals and plays. She worked extensively on stage until joining *Listen With Mother*.

On television, Daphne played a host of characters, including the shopkeeper Mrs Patterson in *To the Manor Born*, Chrissy Plummer's mother in *Man About the House*, Evelyn Spurling in *Land of Hope and Gloria* and Miss Denham in *Fresh Fields*. Her last TV appearance was in a commercial for Sainsbury. Her film appearances have included playing David Essex's mother in *That'll Be the Day* and Jenny Agutter's in the 1980 picture *Sweet William*.

Daphne, who's still working, recorded the annual radio programme *Listen With Les*, with Les Dawson, for fourteen years, and provided the female voice on *What the Papers Say* for thirty-two years.

ROBIN PARKINSON
Role: Desmond
Episode: 'Moonlight and Roses'
Robin left school and worked for his father, a commercial artist, before attending drama school. He entered the business in 1958, appearing in a TV series while finishing his drama studies. Regular TV and film work soon came his way, and he made his big-screen debut in the 1963 movie *Billy Liar*, as a jeweller's assistant. Other film credits include *Twisted Nerve*, *Catch Me a Spy* and *The Family Way*.

He has made numerous TV appearances, including twenty episodes of the 1970s series *The Many Wives of Patrick*, an episode of *Dad's Army*, *The Dick Emery Show*, *Girls About Town*, three series of *'Allo, 'Allo* and an episode of *Outside Edge*.

BRIAN PECK
Role: Ron
Episode: 'Come On In, the Water's Lovely'
Brian, who's also a theatre director, began his career as a child actor in 1946, appearing in children's films. Since graduating from the Webber Douglas Academy in 1952, he's enjoyed a busy career on stage and television. His small-screen credits include *Z Cars, Softly Softly, Dixon of Dock Green, The Brothers, Doomwatch, Coronation Street, Crossroads, Minder, Murder Unproven, The Bill, Boon, Sorry!, Last of the Summer Wine* and *London's Burning*.

JOHN QUAYLE
Role: Groom
Episode: 'Pink Carnations'
John trained at RADA before beginning a career that has taken him around the world. As well as working extensively in the theatre, on television he's played a freelance journalist in *The Good Life*, Major Willoughby-Gore in *Farrington of the FO*, Woodley in *The 19th Hole* and roles in a myriad of other shows, including *Upstairs, Downstairs, Terry and June, Pig in the Middle, Tricky Business, The King's Dragon, Jane* and *Nanny*.

FANNY ROWE
Role: Mother
Episode: 'Come On In, the Water's Lovely'
Fanny was studying at Cambridge when she became involved in acting. Her interest grew so intense she gave up her degree to concentrate on making a career on the stage. She worked in reps around the country and spent much of her early career in the theatre, becoming an accomplished and well-known Shavian actress.

Eventually television work became more prominent in Fanny's career. Her small-screen credits include appearances as Emily Forsyte in the sixties series *The Forsyte Saga*, Mrs Eshton in the 1970 series of *Jane Eyre*, Martha in the 1971 mini-series *Vanity Fair*, Nancy Penrose in *Fresh Fields*, two series of Yorkshire's sitcom *Life Begins At Forty* as Mrs Bunting, *After Henry* and *Upstairs, Downstairs*.

Fanny, who also appeared in several films, died in 1988.

DAVID ROWLANDS

Role: The Curate

Episode: 'Things That Go Bump in the Night'

David won a scholarship to the Guildhall School of Music and Drama at the age of fifteen. He made his TV debut in Rediffusion's *All About You*, before building up a string of small-screen credits in shows like *Doctor Who*, *Are You Being Served?*, *The Fall and Rise of Reginald Perrin*, *The Two Ronnies* and *'Allo, 'Allo*, playing a doctor.

David, who took a break from acting during the mid-1970s to gain a degree in International Relations, also worked for Radio Sussex as a reporter for seven months and qualified as a teacher. Today he works as supply teacher in secondary schools and lives on a farm in west Wales.

ANDREW SACHS

Role: Mr Snell

Episode: 'Great Expectations'

Best known for playing Manuel in *Fawlty Towers*, Andrew was born in Berlin, of parents who fled Nazi Germany and arrived in England with their son when he was just seven. After leaving school he pursued his wish to establish a career in the theatre and spent many years in tours and reps, including Worthing and Liverpool. He has also appeared in the West End.

Andrew's numerous television credits include *Crown Court*, *The Tommy Cooper Show*, *Ask Aspel*, *Strangers*, *The Les Dawson Show*, *The History of Mr Polly* and *The Tempest*. He has also written several stage plays.

JOAN SANDERSON

Role: Mother

Episode: 'Pink Carnations'

Joan was often cast as formidable characters, such as the deaf Mrs Richards in *Fawlty Towers* and Miss Ewell, a teacher in *Please Sir!* A graduate of RADA, she made her stage debut at the Shakespeare Memorial Theatre, Stratford, before moving into rep.

After the Second World War she undertook the first of many visits to the West End stage with *See How They Run*. Her television career began with the 1960s comedy series *All Gas and Gaiters*, before she moved on to *Please Sir!* Other small-screen credits include *Ripping Yarns*, *Upstairs, Downstairs*, *The Other 'Arf*, *Land of Hope and Gloria*, four series of

Me and My Girl and *After Henry.* Joan died at the age of seventy-nine in 1992, shortly after finishing a fifth series of the last-named sitcom.

GEORGE SEWELL
Role: Baker
Episode: 'The Prowler'
Born in 1924, George has been a regular on TV since the 1960s, appearing in many shows, including an episode of *Gideon's Way, Doctor Who* and *Redcap* back in the early sixties. Among his other credits are *Man in a Suitcase, The Adventurer, The Sweeney, The Gentle Touch, Minder, The Upper Hand, Heartbeat* and regular roles as Detective Inspector Brogan in *Z Cars,* Colonel Alec Freeman in *UFO,* Detective Chief Inspector Alan Craven in *Special Branch* and, more recently, Superintendent Cottam in *The Detectives.*

His film work includes such pictures as *Sparrows Can't Sing, This Sporting Life, The Informers, Robbery, Get Carter, Barry Lyndon* and *Operation Daybreak.*

ANTHONY SHARP
Role: De Vere-Brown
Episode: 'Stand Up and Be Counted'
Anthony led a busy acting career before his death in 1984, at the age of sixty-nine.

A regular character player on television, he was seen in numerous productions, including *To the Manor Born, The Young Ones* as Roland Percival, *Keep It in the Family* as Mr Baker, *George and Mildred, Doomwatch, Dad's Army* and *Counterstrike.*

His film career embraced over thirty movies, such as *Teheran, The Sword and the Rose, Left, Right and Centre, Invasion, Rebound, One of Our Dinosaurs is Missing, Never Say Never Again* as Lord Ambrose and *Crossed Swords* as Dr Buttes.

CAMPBELL SINGER
Role: Flint
Episode: 'The Last of the Big Spenders'
Campbell was a busy character actor on both stage and screen, and was also a published author. His television work included playing Henry Burroughs in *The Newcomers,* a porter in *The Persuaders,* several characters in *Doctor Who,* and Colonel Segur in *Danger Man.*

On the big screen he was seen in over fifty pictures, such as *Take My Life, Operation Diamond* as Bert, *The Blue Lamp* as the station sergeant, *Someone at the Door, Cage of Gold* as a policeman, *Pool of London, The Man With the Twisted Lip, Lady in the Fog, The Yellow Balloon* as Potter, *Home at Seven* as Inspector Hemmingway, *Emergency Call, The Titfield Thunderbolt, Street Corner, Conflict of Wings* as Flight Sergeant Campbell and *The Square Peg* as Sergeant Loder.

Campbell died in 1976, aged sixty-seven.

MICHAEL STAINTON
Role: Policeman
Episode: 'The Prowler'
Michael spent the early years of his career on stage, appearing with various rep companies and theatres around the country, but the lion's share of his recent work has been on television. In 1997 he played Edgar Sturgeon in *Dalziel and Pascoe*, while two years earlier he was seen as George in *Prime Suspect*. Other productions include *Jekyll and Hyde, Fellow Traveller, Ever Decreasing Circles, Slinger's Day, Grange Hill, The Manageress, French Fields, Never the Twain, Bread, London's Burning, Birds of a Feather, Pie in the Sky, Only Fools and Horses* and six series of *Metal Mickey*, as the father. The various occasions on which he has played a policeman include an episode of *Juliet Bravo* in 1980.

Michael's theatre work includes productions of *No Sex Please, We're British* and a tour of *Seven-Year Itch*.

MICHAEL WARD
Role: Labour Candidate
Episode: 'Stand Up and Be Counted'
Michael belonged to that clutch of character actors whose services were in such demand during the heyday of the British film industry that they seemed to appear in every post-war movie. He made his name playing small parts throughout the fifties and sixties, in films such as *Tom Brown's Schooldays, The Love Lottery* and *Doctor in Love*, while his more substantial contributions included appearances as Maurice in Norman Wisdom's *Up in the World*, and as Elvin, an ornithologist, in *Sleeping Car to Trieste*.

Michael, whose father was a parish vicar, trained at the Central School of Speech and Drama after a brief stint as a teacher. By the outbreak of the Second World War he'd already made several stage appearances, and he returned to the theatre when the war ended. His film debut in the 1947 picture *The First Gentleman* marked the beginning of a busy career which included appearances in five Norman Wisdom movies and five *Carry On*s. His last film was *Revenge of the Pink Panther*, in which he played an estate agent. On TV, he appeared in shows such as *Morecambe and Wise, Crossroads, Hancock's Half-Hour, The Two Ronnies, Steptoe and Son* and *The New Avengers*.

Ill health forced Michael to retire from acting in 1980. He died in 1997 at the age of eighty-eight.

8

EPISODE GUIDE

Pilot
'The New Tenant' (transmitted 2 September 1974)

Series 1
'Black Magic' (13 December 1974)
'A Night Out' (20 December 1974)
'Charisma' (27 December 1974)
'All Our Yesterdays' (3 January 1975)
'The Prowler' (10 January 1975)
'Stand Up and Be Counted' (17 January 1975)

Series 2
'The Permissive Society' (7 November 1975)
'Food Glorious Food' (14 November 1975)
'A Body Like Mine' (21 November 1975)
'Moonlight and Roses' (28 November 1975)
'A Perfect Gentleman' (5 December 1975)
'The Last of the Big Spenders' (12 December 1975)
'Things That Go Bump in the Night' (19 December 1975)
Christmas Special: 'For the Man Who Has Everything'
(26 December 1975)

Series 3
'That's My Boy' (12 April 1977)
'Stage Struck' (19 April 1977)
'Clunk Click' (26 April 1977)
'The Good Samaritans' (3 May 1977)
'Fawcett's Python' (10 May 1977)

Elizabeth Adare (Lucy in 'For the Man Who Has Everything') also appeared in Eric Chappell's stage play, 'The Banana Box'.

The editor's knife meant we never saw the Peppery Man (James Bree) in 'Clunk Click'.

Suicidal Mr Gray (David Swift) stayed just one night in 'The Good Samaritans'.

Andonia Katsaros played Marilyn, the exotic dancer in 'Fawcett's Python'.

In Rigsby's hour of need, he discovered who his true friends were!

The snooty Caroline (Judy Buxton) made two appearances as Alan's girlfriend.

Robin and Lorna (Alun Lewis and Deborah Watling) booked in at Rigsby's for a night of passion in 'Hello, Young Lovers'.

The late Robert Dorning (back row, left) played Lorna's father in 'Hello, Young Lovers'.

Theology student Gwyn Williams (John Clive) arrived in 'Fire and Brimstone'.

Rigsby caused mayhem in 'Pink Carnations'.

The late Peter Jeffrey played a so-called mystic in 'Under the Influence'.

Alan and Philip became best mates.

The opinionated Rupert Rigsby's dress sense left a lot to be desired.

Life was pretty cramped in Rigsby's lodging house.

Rigsby saw himself as something of a father-figure for Alan.

Rigsby doted on Miss Jones who did her best to tolerate his overbearing attentions.

Sadly, Miss Jones was never to walk down the aisle.

'The Cocktail Hour' (17 May 1977)
'Suddenly at Home' (24 May 1977)

Series 4

'Hello Young Lovers' (4 April 1978)
'Fire and Brimstone' (11 April 1978)
'Great Expectations' (18 April 1978)
'Pink Carnations' (25 April 1978)
'Under the Influence' (2 May 1978)
'Come On In, the Water's Lovely' (9 May 1978)

PILOT
'The New Tenant' (also known as 'Rooksby')

Rehearsals: St Paul's Church Hall, Sussex Place, London W6
Recorded: 7 July 1974
First transmission: 2 September 1974

Leonard Rossiter . . . . Rigsby
Richard Beckinsale . . . . Alan
Frances de la Tour . . . . Ruth
Don Warrington . . . . Philip

There's a spare room in the house and Alan, who lives in the frozen attic, wants it. But Rigsby wants to go upmarket and attract a member of the professional class. However, when Miss Jones asks whether a student friend from the nearby college can move in, Rigsby – who would do anything for his beloved Ruth – is prepared to let him rent the room for £4 a week.

Alan finds his room stripped of furniture, in preparation for the 'gentleman's' visit, but the new lodger isn't what the prejudice-laden Rigsby expected. Keen to see him on his way as soon as possible, he tries putting him off the room with tales of weak walls and gas that hisses like a snake. But his efforts are in vain because Philip is happy with the room – that is, until Miss Jones welcomes him with an impulsive kiss on the sofa, and everyone keeps barging in uninvited, disrupting his studies.

Just as Philip begins packing his bags, Rigsby – who realizes he'll upset Miss Jones if he forces him out – tells him not to be hasty and directs him to the attic, where he tries selling the new tenant the idea of sharing a room with Alan.

SERIES 1

1. 'Black Magic'

Rehearsals: St Paul's Church Hall, Sussex Place, London W6
Recorded: 3 November 1974
First transmission: 13 December 1974

Leonard Rossiter . . . . Rigsby
Richard Beckinsale . . . . Alan
Frances de la Tour . . . . Ruth
Don Warrington . . . . Philip

The new tenant causes much interest in the household: while Miss Jones fantasizes about starting a relationship with Philip, Alan and Rigsby can't believe he's the son of an African chief and has ten wives. And when Philip casually informs his landlord that he's a god and has inherited supernatural powers, Rigsby continues making sarcastic comments. Philip switches off the lights, turns to his spear and ceremonial headdress and summons up the spirits. Rigsby takes some convincing; he thinks it's all in the mind, even though he nearly breaks his leg on the stairs after leaving their room. But he's not entirely dismissive of the idea of conjuring up psychic powers and when he finds himself alone in Alan and Philip's room for a moment he picks up Philip's spear, taps the floorboards and waits. What he doesn't realize is that he's being watched, not by spirits but by his laughing lodgers.

2. 'A Night Out'

Rehearsals: St Paul's Church Hall, Sussex Place, London W6
Recorded: 17 November 1974
First transmission: 20 December 1974

Leonard Rossiter . . . . Rigsby
Richard Beckinsale . . . . Alan
Frances de la Tour . . . . Ruth
Don Warrington . . . . Philip
Derek Newark . . . . Spooner
Frank Gatliff . . . . Manager
Extras: Tom Growlin, Penelope Carlisle, Sylvia Stoker, Patrick Lynas, Douglas Quaterman, Norah Blackman, Mark Freeman, Yvonne Sommerling, Stuart Teal, Tom Harrison, Martin le Roy.
Walk-ons: Peter Newton, Mike Thorley, Alan Frith, Fenella Stone, Conrad Vince, Carl Rae, Angela Elliott, Winifred Williams, Lisa Anning, Joanne Aspey.

Rigsby is dressed up to the nines, although his pinstriped suit (one of Spooner's cast-offs), a white silk scarf and gloves raise a smile on Alan and Philip's faces. The motive behind Rigsby's incongruous attire is that it's Miss Jones's birthday and as she's only received two cards he wants to cheer her up. Rigsby plans taking her to The Grange, one of the finest restaurants in the area, but not before he ditches the pinstripes and raids Spooner's wardrobe for a more suitable jacket while the wrestler is away.

At The Grange, puffing on a huge cigar, Rigsby tries turning on the charm towards Miss Jones, but loses out to Philip on the first dance. Rigsby's annoyance at his lodger for not taking the hint and leaving the way open for him to pursue Miss Jones is quickly replaced by fright when Spooner – who hates anyone borrowing his clothes – arrives at the restaurant.

While Rigsby hides behind a menu, Spooner spots Alan wearing his favourite bow tie and rips it from around his neck. Thinking he's escaped the attention of the wrestler, Rigsby continues with the objective of the evening and invites Miss Jones to waltz; but trouble brews when Spooner confronts him about wearing his suit and ends up ripping the sleeves off. To top it all, Rigsby is landed with a whopping bill and thrown off the premises. Not a birthday to remember for poor Miss Jones.

3. 'Charisma'
Rehearsals: St Paul's Church Hall, Sussex Place, London W6
Recorded: 10 November 1974
First transmission: 27 December 1974

Leonard Rossiter	Rigsby
Richard Beckinsale	Alan
Frances de la Tour	Ruth
Don Warrington	Philip
Liz Edmiston	Maureen

While mending her leaking tap, Rigsby tells Miss Jones she has brought a touch of refinement to the house, what with shades on the bulbs and blue water in the toilet. Before leaving he invites her to a wrestling match and a spot of supper afterwards, but she turns him down with a weak excuse about having to work late.

Upstairs, Alan and Philip moan about being not allowed to bring girls back to the room. Alan believes the only way around Rigsby is to pair him off with Miss Jones, even though the chances of that happening are minimal. When Rigsby turns up and tells them Miss Jones has spurned him again, Alan offers some advice. He feels Rigsby needs a little charisma, and what Miss Jones really wants is a quiet evening in listening to Matt Monro. With the help of Philip's medallion, Alan's LP and his relaxation pills, Rigsby feels ready for the challenge, although what Alan forgot to tell him is that the pills will turn his water green!

With his shirt buttons undone to his navel, the 'medallion man' sways into Miss Jones's room, and with the pills beginning to kick in, he fails to notice he's put the record on the wrong speed; as the vocals struggle out of the record player the evening turns into a failure.

In desperation Rigsby turns to Philip for advice, and is gullible enough to fall for his tale that burning the wood of the love tree in her presence would soon have her falling for him. After plucking up enough courage to give it a try, Rigsby gets more than he bargained for when Miss Jones ends up extinguishing his stick, drenching him in the process.

When Philip arrives back at the house and, unaware that Rigsby's evening has been a complete failure, asks the sodden landlord whether he can bring a girl up to his room, he suffers the sharp end of Rigsby's tongue.

4. 'All Our Yesterdays'
Rehearsals: St Paul's Church Hall, Sussex Place, London W6
Recorded: 24 November 1974
First transmission: 3 January 1975

Leonard Rossiter . . . . Rigsby
Richard Beckinsale . . . . Alan
Frances de la Tour . . . . Ruth
Don Warrington . . . . Philip
Derek Newark . . . . Spooner

Spooner's music has been blaring all evening and is driving everyone mad, but no one is brave enough to confront him because he's been in a foul mood ever since he tripped over Vienna, tumbled down the stairs and broke his leg. Rigsby reluctantly accepts responsibility and agrees to tell the wrestler to turn the volume down, but they end up arguing over Vienna's role in the accident and Rigsby rushes out of the room without mentioning the noise.

In Alan and Philip's room, questions about bravery and Rigsby's dubious war record arise, but Rigsby claims to possess braveheart courage, even if he quakes at the thought of telling Spooner about his radio. When Philip doubts his war record Rigsby fetches his mementoes from five years of conflict to show the lads, but soon realizes neither of them is interested.

When Spooner, who's getting increasingly drunk, starts singing at the top of his voice, Rigsby sees no option but to confront him, but again fails to resolve the matter.

Later, when Alan – after donning a German soldier's jacket – larks around with an old gun, Rigsby accidentally pulls the trigger and finds a bullet, left in the gun by mistake, has gone straight through Spooner's door. Deciding to get his own back on the miserly landlord, the wrestler plays dead while Rigsby suffers.

5. 'The Prowler'

Rehearsals: St Paul's Church Hall, Sussex Place, London W6
Recorded: 1 December 1974
First transmission: 10 January 1975

Leonard Rossiter . . . . Rigsby
Richard Beckinsale. . . . . Alan
Frances de la Tour . . . . Ruth
Don Warrington. . . . . Philip
George Sewell. . . . . Baker
Michael Stainton. . . . . Policeman

Extra: Kelwyn Harrison – Non-Speaking Policeman

When screams are heard from Miss Jones's room, Rigsby is soon on the scene, although he's surprised to hear she's seen a prowler staring through the window, because her room is high up and there's no drain-pipe. Taking advantage of the situation, Rigsby suggests he stays by her side all night.

Suddenly a policeman arrives on the scene, even though no one called for help, explaining that he's investigating a reported prowler. He interviews everyone in the house and warns them that 'we're in greater danger from the people we know'. When Miss Jones picks out Rigsby during a makeshift identity parade (Alan and Philip were the only others in the line) the policeman's attention focuses on Rigsby's movements that evening.

Rigsby feels he's been grilled, but when the supposed policeman takes a different stance and informs him that he could tell by his face that he was an honest man, Rigsby is fooled and allows him to search the house before leaving.

Later, when real police officers arrive and explain they're on the hunt for a bogus policeman, Rigsby discovers his money box has been stolen.

6. 'Stand Up and Be Counted'

Rehearsals: St Paul's Church Hall, Sussex Place, London W6
Recorded: 8 December 1974
First transmission: 17 January 1975

Leonard Rossiter	Rigsby
Richard Beckinsale	Alan
Frances de la Tour	Ruth
Don Warrington	Philip
Michael Ward	Labour Candidate
Ian Lavender	Platt
Anthony Sharp	De Vere-Brown

It's election time and Rigsby's sporting the blue rosette of the Tories, while Alan accuses him of being a social climber. Keen to gain more friends at the local Conservative Club because the only person who speaks to him at the moment washes the glasses, Rigsby agrees to do some canvassing for the party.

Alan and Philip are voting Labour, but Miss Jones is an undecided voter, swaying from one party to the next, depending on which candidate she likes the look of most. Rigsby pops in to try and persuade her to vote for the Blues, but when young Mr Platt, the Liberal candidate, visits, she's tempted to vote for him because of his 'lovely smile'.

A knock at the door finds Colonel De Vere-Brown, the Tory candidate, on the doorstep, making Rigsby's evening, until one of his dogs dirties the carpet. But worse is to follow when the snooty De Vere-Brown criticizes the house, claiming 'it's the unacceptable face of capitalism', especially with the damp. If he gets elected he promises to pull down buildings like Rigsby's. An argument ensues and Rigsby throws him out before donning the red of Labour.

SERIES 2

1. 'Permissive Society'

Rehearsals: Sulgrave Boys' Club, 287 Goldhawk Road, London W12
Recorded: 25 July 1975
First transmission: 7 November 1975

Leonard Rossiter . . . . Rigsby
Richard Beckinsale . . . . Alan
Frances de la Tour . . . . Ruth
Don Warrington . . . . Philip
George A. Cooper . . . . Cooper

Philip has arranged a blind date for Alan to help make up a foursome. Before they go out Rigsby pops up and the three start chatting about love and erogenous zones, even though Rigsby believes they're somewhere near the equator! Before he returns to his own room, he reminds the lads that the permissive society stops outside the door; he doesn't want it entering his house.

The boys' evening is a wash-out, thanks largely to Alan, who Philip feels is afraid of women and a little immature. Next day he persuades Alan to practise his technique on Miss Jones, but just as the young medical student enters her bedroom, with Miss Jones asleep in bed, Mr Rigsby bursts in. Alan dives into the wardrobe as Rigsby spurts out a myriad of chat-up lines, but when he spots a dressing-gown cord being pulled through the cupboard door, he can't believe it when he finds Alan inside.

Playing Sandra's Father

George A. Cooper, who played the father of Alan's unseen girlfriend, Sandra, feels there is no finer example of perfect casting and writing coming together than in *Rising Damp*. 'It was absolutely spot-on; in terms of audience appeal I think the only one that compares with it for richness of dialogue is *Only Fools and Horses*. Although I only appeared in one episode, it was terrific fun.'

2. 'Food Glorious Food'

Rehearsals: Sulgrave Boys' Club, 287 Goldhawk Road, London W12
Recorded: 18 July 1975
First transmission: 14 November 1975

Leonard Rossiter . . . . Rigsby
Richard Beckinsale . . . . Alan
Frances de la Tour . . . . Ruth
Don Warrington . . . . Philip

Miss Jones is on the prowl with her collecting tin, so Rigsby rushes up to Alan's flat. He claims he's skint but when he hears her climbing the stairs he hides behind a curtain. Miss Jones soon spots Rigsby, who agrees to donate, although it's debatable whether it is a spare button or a copper he hurriedly pushes into the tin.

When Philip arrives there is a heated debate about droughts and famines, with Rigsby claiming that he went without food for a whole week when he was in the desert; Philip doesn't think Rigsby could manage without food for forty-eight hours, let alone a week, and bets him £5.

Rigsby's eyes light up at the thought of earning a fiver and starts planning what he'll spend the money on. Although he claims it's all about will power, Rigsby starts getting edgy after forty-five minutes, and is struggling when Alan, who's keeping an eye on him, starts eating sweets. Things gets rough when Miss Jones delivers some spare fish for Vienna: Rigsby's eyes nearly pop out of his head, but before he can get his teeth into his unexpected meal, Philip arrives on the scene.

Rigsby gets himself into a right state and even believes he's contracted rickets. He tries blackmailing Alan by saying he'll split the fiver in return for a few sausages, and they won't even have to meet: Alan can just leave something on a plate outside his door. When he later finds a plate of food left outside he thinks Alan has agreed to his idea, not realizing that the plate contains scraps for Vienna.

At the end of the forty-eight hours, a high-spirited Rigsby triumphantly collects his fiver from Philip. But his joy is short-lived: when Miss Jones sees him holding the money, she thinks he's going to donate it to Famine Relief and grabs it. To cap it all, he discovers the food he's eaten was the week's leftovers.

3. 'A Body Like Mine'
Rehearsals: Sulgrave Boys' Club, 287 Goldhawk Road, London W12
Recorded: 1 August 1975
First transmission: 21 November 1975

Leonard Rossiter . . . . Rigsby
Richard Beckinsale . . . . Alan
Frances de la Tour . . . . Ruth
Don Warrington . . . . Philip

Miss Jones has taken up exercise to improve her figure, although Rigsby doesn't feel there's any need. He tells her he's a little fed up with all the keep-fit campaigns going on inside the household and feels such pre-occupation with the physique is unnecessary.

When Rigsby sees Alan and Philip they discuss exercising and Rigsby claims Alan was meant to be puny and believes he's fitter and stronger than him any day. When Miss Jones cries for help because she wants a pickle jar opened, and Alan hasn't the strength, Rigsby steps in. But he's embarrassed because it's beyond his capabilities, and it's left for Philip to open the jar with ease.

Rigsby decides to reclaim some credibility in the eyes of Miss Jones. He boasts about his prowess at soccer and boxing, and says that if he had another pair of gloves he'd prove something to Philip; what he didn't expect was that Philip would take him up on his offer.

That evening Rigsby turns white when he hears Philip was regional champion back in Africa. He tries getting out of the boxing match without losing face, but it's too late. It's a decrepit-looking Rigsby who steps into the ring, but Philip takes a dive in order to lose the winning prize of taking Miss Jones out for a meal.

4. 'Moonlight and Roses'
Rehearsals: Sulgrave Boys' Club, 287 Goldhawk Road, London W12
Recorded: 19 September 1975
First transmission: 28 November 1975

Leonard Rossiter . . . . Rigsby
Richard Beckinsale . . . . Alan
Frances de la Tour . . . . Ruth
Don Warrington . . . . Philip
Robin Parkinson . . . . Desmond
Gay Rose . . . . Brenda

Love is in the air for Miss Jones, but as she stands on the doorstep kissing her new lover, librarian Desmond, Alan spies on them from the window, just in case he hears a good chat-up line from the poetry-spouting Desmond, who wants to take Miss Jones far away from the squalor of her bedsit.

Rigsby, unaware that Miss Jones is on the doorstep with her new flame, asks Philip and Alan whether they've noticed a change in her. He says all her 'mooning around', sighing and extra dabs of scent are signs that she's finally fallen for him, but then he notices Desmond from the window with his arms entwined around Miss Jones. When Miss Jones comes in singing, Rigsby realizes things are serious.

The following evening, Miss Jones accepts Desmond's proposal of marriage but tries to keep her decision quiet, fearing that Rigsby will cut her water off. But when she hardly has time to talk to Rigsby any more, he realizes he's got to do something before he loses her for ever. Philip

Playing Desmond

Robin Parkinson played drippy Desmond, Miss Jones's intended, in just one episode. But the popularity of the sitcom means people are still reminding the actor, some twenty-five years later.

'I was working in the theatre recently and was in the bar after the performance when somebody turned to me and said: "I remember you played Miss Jones's fiancé in *Rising Damp*." The series holds up very well and I still watch the repeats, it's a marvellous sitcom.

'When I think about why the show worked, I think the success is largely due to the little tight-knit cast; they played off each other so well, although the centrepiece was Leonard Rossiter's performance. I sit in awe of him, he was fantastic. I regard him as the best comedy actor this country has produced in the last thirty or forty years. He was wonderful to work with, and he makes his performances seem effortless, even though he'd put so much time and hard work into the job. That's the sign of a very good actor.

'When it came to playing Desmond I didn't have to think too much about it because the scripts were so well written the character just came off the page.'

suggests some chat-up lines Rigsby might use, but what he doesn't tell him is that they've been pinched from the mouth of Desmond. Miss Jones is furious when Rigsby tries the lines out on her, accuses him of eavesdropping on her private conversations and sends him packing.

When Rigsby tries apologizing to Miss Jones next day, he finds her bags packed. Drastic action is required, so when he manages to get Desmond on his own, he states Miss Jones is an alcoholic and a violent woman afraid of men. Desmond runs out in panic.

But it's not long before the librarian returns, proclaiming he'll have Miss Jones, warts and all. It's the end of an era in Rigsby's household as Miss Jones leaves, although he's quick to offer the room to the curvaceous Brenda, a friend of Alan's, who he sees as the ideal replacement for Miss Jones.

5. 'A Perfect Gentleman'
Rehearsals: Sulgrave Boys' Club, 287 Goldhawk Road, London W12
Recorded: 10 October 1975
First transmission: 5 December 1975

Leonard Rossiter	Rigsby
Richard Beckinsale	Alan
Don Warrington	Philip
Henry McGee	Seymour

A new tenant, Seymour, fools the credulous Rigsby into thinking he's a financially astute member of society. Rigsby is so taken in he ends up cleaning Seymour's shoes, lets him stay in the bath for hours and doesn't press him for rent. Alan and Philip, meanwhile, see the newcomer for what he is: a scrounging con man, who's out to rip off fools like Rigsby before moving on to pastures – and pockets – new.

When Philip mislays his wallet, he suspects Seymour, and he, Alan and Rigsby check his room. Seymour returns and insists that, as he is the chief suspect, they search him. In turn he suggests everyone else is searched, and when a wallet is found on Alan, no one can believe it – except Seymour, who planted it.

Seymour's next target is Rigsby, and he nabs his purse. Rigsby accuses Alan, but Philip defends his friend and says he'll prove it wasn't him. When Seymour, claiming that the mayor is to visit, borrows £30 to buy some champagne and takes Rigsby's money belt in the process, Philip catches him and exposes Seymour for what he is: a cad.

The Gasman Cometh

Robert Gillespie is a regular in the world of television sitcom, often hired to play, in his words, 'quirky characters'. The Gasman in 'The Last of the Big Spenders' was right up Robert's street.

'There is a wonderful story behind the scene where the money falls out of Rigsby's pocket when he's just told the gasman he hasn't a penny. Leonard never played the "star", but he always knew what he wanted and this scene is no exception because the way the money fell out of his pockets was his idea.

'Leonard felt the way it was planned in the script was very tame and wouldn't generate the sort of laughs he wanted; Rigsby was a nervous, jumpy sort of character, so Len suggested that just as he thinks he's getting away with it, the coins start coming out of his trouser leg; he wanted a slit in the pocket in which he would hold the money. At just the right moment he would push his hand through the slit and release the coins. In the other pocket, where the money just pours out, he wanted a little wooden box which he'd empty. To create the tension he wanted to let the coins trickle out at first, before they flooded out of the other pocket. We then found that the coins were falling on to the studio floor but making no sound whatsoever, so he had a special board made out of plywood to make a loud, rattling noise.

'Very few comic actors bother going into that kind of detail, but the great ones do. When it came to recording, we didn't have to do a single retake. The credit for that brilliant piece of physical comedy is entirely down to Leonard.

'In my view, *Rising Damp* worked because Eric Chappell got the balance of characters right and delivered good scripts, with the cast making them work. Leonard was just excellent: he had a particular line of comedy which was unusual in this country, a highly satirical edge, which you find much more in French actors. He was an absolute perfectionist who worked and worked. Through his performance he would tell the audience that he was playing a character he wanted them to look at, whether they agreed with him or not.'

6. 'The Last of the Big Spenders'

Rehearsals: Sulgrave Boys' Club, 287 Goldhawk Road, London W12
Recorded: 17 October 1975
First transmission: 12 December 1975

Leonard Rossiter . . . . Rigsby
Richard Beckinsale . . . . Alan
Don Warrington . . . . Philip
Gay Rose . . . . Brenda
Campbell Singer . . . . Flint
Robert Gillespie . . . . Gasman
Ronnie Brody . . . . Charlie

Rigsby has splashed out on some new, gaudy furniture but is too mean to lend Alan a fiver when he asks, telling him that if he's desperate he can retrieve the 50p that's fallen down the back of one of his chairs.

When Brenda pops in to see Rigsby they get talking about style and he makes out he doesn't flinch when it comes to throwing his money around. Brenda gets the wrong end of the stick and thinks Rigsby has offered to take her out for a tasty dinner, and he has no option but to try scrounging money off Philip, but he won't have anything to do with it. Rigsby is reduced to raiding the gas meters, but finds himself in trouble when the gasman comes to cut off his supply. He pleads poverty, and with no pension and his shrapnel playing up, he tries desperately to eke out a little sympathy from the gasman. Just when it appears he's won the day, they shake hands and all the coppers pour from his pockets.

When Brenda pops down, ready for the evening meal, Rigsby says he can't go because Vienna is ill. He persuades her to eat in, slips on his smoking jacket and is ready to entertain, but a knock on the door brings the bailiffs, who have arrived to reclaim the furniture as he hasn't paid the bill.

7. 'Things That Go Bump in the Night'

Rehearsals: Sulgrave Boys' Club, 287 Goldhawk Road, London W12
Recorded: 24 October 1975
First transmission: 19 December 1975

Leonard Rossiter . . . . Rigsby
Richard Beckinsale . . . . Alan

Don Warrington . . . . Philip
Gay Rose . . . . Brenda
Norman Bird . . . . Vicar
David Rowlands . . . . Curate

Brenda and Alan return from seeing *Doctor Zhivago* at the pictures, but when he tells Rigsby, who's been waiting for him like an over-concerned father, he thinks the doctor was a real medic whom Alan had consulted about his prickly heat.

Later Rigsby tries frightening Alan by suggesting the house is haunted. He tells the lads about the grey lady who's supposed to roam the place at night; when he's gone, Philip suggests giving Rigsby a taste of his own medicine.

When Rigsby comes out of Brenda's room he sees the figure of a woman dressed in grey and is so frightened he races up to Philip's room. When he finally plucks up enough courage to head downstairs again he bumps into the bonneted lady once more.

Even though Rigsby calls in the local vicar to help, Philip suggests the only way to understand and, hopefully, rid the house of the grey lady is to hold a séance. Philip, Rigsby and Brenda hold hands as they try to make contact with the apparition. When Rigsby realizes it's Alan larking about, he's determined to seek his revenge, but ends up embarrassing himself in front of the vicar.

Playing the Curate

Around the time of his appearance as the curate in 'Things That Go Bump in the Night', David Rowlands found himself being offered lots of roles as a churchman.

'I was always being offered either clerical roles or upper-class characters, I don't know why. Leonard Rossiter was very helpful; he was unlike any other comedy actor, or comedian, I had worked with because he was so unselfish: he was happy to help others get the laugh.'

CHRISTMAS SPECIAL
'For the Man Who Has Everything'

Rehearsals: Sulgrave Boys' Club, 287 Goldhawk Road, London W12
Recorded: 19 December 1975
First transmission: 26 December 1975

Leonard Rossiter	Rigsby
Richard Beckinsale	Alan
Don Warrington	Philip
Gay Rose	Brenda
Larry Martyn	Fred
Elizabeth Adare	Lucy
Helen Fraser	Gwen

It's Boxing Day, but with all his tenants away, Rigsby hasn't got anyone to share it with, except Vienna. When the milkman delivers the milk but hasn't got any double cream left, Rigsby believes it's because he didn't give him a Christmas box. The milkman feels insulted and tells Rigsby he can understand why he's spending the festive period alone.

Thinking Rigsby was spending Christmas with his brother, Alan returns early with Brenda. While Brenda takes a bath, Alan pops down to borrow the electric fire, and is shocked to see Rigsby. They get chatting and Rigsby admits it was miserable spending Christmas Day alone, partly because he didn't have anyone to pull the wishbone with. Alan jokes that at least he got the wish, but Rigsby remarks that it hasn't come true because he wished for a nubile young lady wearing a negligee. When Brenda arrives after her bath, Rigsby feels his wish has come true. He dolls himself up, brushes his hair, fancies his chances and heads up to get his promised Christmas kiss for unblocking her drains earlier in the year.

Philip arrives with his girlfriend, Lucy, hoping that she can rent a room for a few days. Knowing Rigsby's views about bringing girls back to the house, he drops in on the landlord and jollies him up by saying his Christmas present is waiting for him in the next room; when he spots Lucy, Rigsby is ecstatic over Philip's generosity, thinking the girl is for him, but he's in for a shock.

SERIES 3
1. 'That's My Boy'
Rehearsals: Sulgrave Boys' Club, 287 Goldhawk Road, London W12
Recorded: 25 March 1977
First transmission: 12 April 1977

Leonard Rossiter . . . . Rigsby
Richard Beckinsale . . . . Alan
Frances de la Tour . . . . Ruth
Don Warrington . . . . Philip
Ann Beach . . . . Mrs Brent
David Daker . . . . Mr Brent
Daphne Oxenford . . . Radio Announcer

Rigsby's back early from his holiday on the Costa Brava, partly because he spent the last three days locked up in a police cell for causing trouble and pushing a German into the pool. While he was away, Alan took it upon himself to let the two empty rooms to two women: Mrs Brent and Miss Jones, who's returned to the squalid conditions because her wedding plans fell apart.

What Alan didn't tell Rigsby was that Mrs Brent has a baby. While she is out trying to find permanent accommodation, Alan agrees to look after the baby but when Rigsby hears it crying he says he can't stand the noise and they'll have to go. Alan persuades Miss Jones to look after it, but Rigsby gets the wrong end of the stick and ends up believing it's her child.

While Miss Jones goes out, Rigsby babysits, but the tot won't stop crying, even though he enacts scenes from children's radio, pretending to be a big, bouncy ball and Rover the dog. When the father – who's in the Merchant Navy – arrives, a case of mistaken identity finds Rigsby in all sorts of problems.

2. 'Stage Struck'
Rehearsals: Sulgrave Boys' Club, 287 Goldhawk Road, London W12
Recorded: 1 April 1977
First transmission: 19 April 1977

Leonard Rossiter . . . . Rigsby
Richard Beckinsale . . . . Alan
Frances de la Tour . . . . Ruth
Don Warrington . . . . Philip
Peter Bowles . . . . Hilary

The cravat-wearing Hilary, an actor who spends more time 'resting' than working, has convinced Alan to play the male lead (Slim) in his new play. When Rigsby discovers there is love interest in the script and Miss Jones is playing Maggie, the female lead, his ears prick up.

Rigsby bursts into Hilary's room during a rehearsal of an intimate love scene, spots Alan with his arms around Miss Jones and pulls him off. Realizing they were only play-acting, the crisp-munching Rigsby decides to stay and watch the rest of the performance, making Alan nervous in the process. When the landlord criticizes the student's attempt at kissing, Hilary watches his male lead storm off in a huff.

Rigsby wants to get in on the act, especially if it involves intimate scenes with Miss Jones, so tries his best to dissuade Alan from taking part by suggesting Hilary is gay. When Hilary gets wind of the fact Rigsby is putting it about that he's limp-wristed he lets Rigsby audition for the part of Slim. What Rigsby doesn't realize is that Hilary knows what he's been up to and decides to play along with the game by playing the female lead! When the scene requires a little cuddling on the sofa, Rigsby is out the door at breakneck speed, leaving Hilary to have the last laugh.

3. 'Clunk Click'
Rehearsals: Sulgrave Boys' Club, 287 Goldhawk Road, London W12
Recorded: 15 April 1977
First transmission: 26 April 1977

Leonard Rossiter	Rigsby
Richard Beckinsale	Alan
Frances de la Tour	Ruth
Don Warrington	Philip
Derek Francis	Mr French
James Bree	Peppery Man
Judy Buxton	Caroline

Alan Takes a Trip!

During the scene in which Alan and Philip rush out of the garage, if you watch carefully you'll notice Richard Beckinsale accidentally trip and bump into the garage door.

Rigsby has bought a sports car and hopes it will help his campaign to woo Miss Jones. And when she accepts his invitation to a do at the country club, he starts thinking his luck may be in, especially as he intends running out of petrol *en route.*

When they return from their evening out, with branches entangled in the car, it's obvious something has gone wrong. Rigsby's reckless driving saw them fly over a humpback bridge, while Miss Jones saw her life flash before her. With a collision also thrown in, she declares he should be banned from the road.

The following day Philip tells Rigsby a man popped round to see him and will call again later. When he hears the man's car had a bumper missing, Rigsby becomes worried that it's the driver whose vehicle he bumped. He receives a further shock when he spots something furry under his own back wheels and believes he's run over Vienna. He asks Philip to put the body into a sack for him, but doesn't realize that it's only Miss Jones's fox fur.

While Rigsby cradles his sack of fur, Alan returns and is told about Vienna's tragic demise. Just as Rigsby heads off to bury the cat, the old man with the missing bumper pulls up and asks for the owner of the

Playing Caroline

Alan's toffee-nosed girlfriend, Caroline Armitage, was played by Judy Buxton. She first appeared in 'Clunk Click' and was seen again in 'The Cocktail Hour', later in the third series, although a different character was originally penned for this episode. So successful had Judy been in bringing Caroline to life, it was decided she should return to the series as the same character.

'There was more to do in the second episode, which was great. She was a very posh character and although I hadn't played such roles before *Rising Damp*, I have done since. I was thrilled to be working with Leonard and Richard, they were fabulous. Leonard was a true perfectionist. He was wonderful to watch in rehearsals because he was so precise in everything; he had every little movement off to a tee – I admired him for that. It was a bit nerve-racking working with him, but I'm glad I had the opportunity.'

sports car. Rigsby denies everything, but when he accidentally pulls off the sheet draping the car, the old man is anxious to meet the owner and says he'll come back at 7pm.

Alan, who'd like to borrow the sports car, shows it off to his new girl-friend, the toffee-nosed Caroline, trying to impress her by suggesting it's his. Although he'd previously refused Alan use of the car, Rigsby – who's worried about the old man's return – tells him he can have it. But when the old man turns up and confesses to being in the wrong over last night's collision and offers £10 settlement, Alan is more than satisfied, jumps in the sports car and tears off.

All that's left for Rigsby to do is cremate Vienna. It's a sad moment as he places the furry thing in the burner, but when Vienna suddenly turns up, the hunt is on for Miss Jones's fox fur.

4. 'The Good Samaritans'
Rehearsals: Sulgrave Boys' Club, 287 Goldhawk Road, London W12
Recorded: 15 April 1977
First transmission: 3 May 1977

Leonard Rossiter	Rigsby
Richard Beckinsale	Alan
Frances de la Tour	Ruth
Don Warrington	Philip
David Swift	Mr Gray
John Clive	Samaritan

Extras: Buddy Prince and Derek Suthern – Stretcher-bearers

It's late at night when Rigsby lets a room to Mr Gray, a dishevelled charac-ter who feels he's sunk to the bottom of society in ending up at a place like Rigsby's. He breaks down and complains about having once lived a life of luxury, eating at the Ritz and associating with the rich. Although the old man is a candidate for suicide, Rigsby is blind to his desperation and leaves him to write farewell letters, believing he's preparing to emigrate.

Discussing the matter with Alan, Rigsby confirms Mr Gray arrived without any luggage and seemed depressed: Alan fears he's going to do himself in, but the unsympathetic Rigsby hopes not because he's just shampooed the carpet. When Philip tells them he's lent Mr Gray his razor, Rigsby nearly does his nut, until Philip mentions it's only electric.

Rigsby decides to see how he's getting on, but soon wishes he hadn't when Mr Gray grabs him and confides that his problems in life are due to a woman who took him for every penny he had. When he finally escapes, Rigsby rushes to Miss Jones and persuades her to speak with Mr Gray to see if she can cheer him up.

Rigsby rings the Samaritans for help, but when a man arrives he ends up mistaking Miss Jones, whom he catches with her head in the oven, and a frenzied Rigsby, who's just finished reading a note from Mr Gray, who's climbed on to the roof, as the victims. Rigsby has no time to mess about, and clambers on to the roof to try and talk Mr Gray down. But before the night is out, Rigsby finds himself being stretchered away to hospital courtesy of the good Samaritan.

5. 'Fawcett's Python'
Rehearsals: Sulgrave Boys' Club, 287 Goldhawk Road, London W12
Recorded: 29 April 1977
First transmission: 10 May 1977

Leonard Rossiter . . . . Rigsby
Richard Beckinsale . . . . Alan
Frances de la Tour . . . . Ruth
Don Warrington . . . . Philip
Andonia Katsaros . . . . Marilyn
Jonathan Elsom . . . . Douglas

A new lodger, Marilyn, moves in and Miss Jones feels the moral climate of the household has nosedived since her arrival; with the curate coming that evening to rehearse for the forthcoming concert, she is worried he'll think she's unfit to take to the church stage.

Although the men in the house are smitten by the new tenant, Rigsby realizes how upset Miss Jones is and decides Marilyn will have to leave, especially when he starts thinking she's a prostitute. He breaks the news to the blonde, brassy negligee-wearing Marilyn, but when he discovers she's only an exotic dancer he reconsiders and allows her to stay. What he didn't realize was that she has brought a pet snake with her, and the sight of Charlie the python sends Rigsby scampering from her room.

When Philip sees the snake he grasps the opportunity to frighten Rigsby by telling him it's a highly dangerous Fawcett's python. Rigsby tells Marilyn that the snake must go, only to find he's already gone and is somewhere in the garden.

When the curate visits Miss Jones that evening, Rigsby has a bright idea. He borrows Philip's stuffed snake with the intention of frightening the churchman away, but his childish prank backfires.

6. 'The Cocktail Hour'

Rehearsals: Sulgrave Boys' Club, 287 Goldhawk Road, London W12
Recorded: 6 May 1977
First transmission: 17 May 1977

> Leonard Rossiter. . . . . Rigsby
> Richard Beckinsale. . . . . Alan
> Frances de la Tour. . . . . Ruth
> Don Warrington. . . . . Philip
> Judy Buxton. . . . . Caroline
> Diana King. . . . . Mrs Armitage

Alan wants to bring his latest girlfriend, Caroline, around to the bedsit but Rigsby won't allow it. As it's Rigsby's night at bingo, Alan takes a chance, but what he doesn't realize is that the landlord has decided to stay at home.

When he learns from Miss Jones that Alan's girlfriend is none other than Caroline Armitage, whose mother is president of the Women's Guild and whose father owns most of the property in the area, Rigsby decides to make an allowance this time.

Upstairs, Caroline is fed up after sitting on a spring amid scenes of decay in Alan's room. And to top it all she ends up lying on a discarded jam sandwich, which leaves a nasty stain on her skirt. While Miss Jones takes care of Caroline and the stain, Rigsby tries giving Alan some advice on social graces, but to no avail, because he continues slurping his tea and dunking his biscuits.

Alan has arranged a cocktail party, to which his prospective mother-in-law has been invited. But one person who hasn't been asked is Rigsby, and when he finds out he takes revenge by gatecrashing the event, donning a party hat and embarrassing Alan by telling him he's left rings around the bath. If that wasn't enough, he accuses Mrs Armitage of being a troublemaker before recognizing her as Mavis Bagworthy, who used to have a runny nose and revealed her knickers to everyone at school. Rigsby's unwelcome outburst brings the evening, and Alan's relationship, to an abrupt end.

7. 'Suddenly at Home'

Rehearsals: Sulgrave Boys' Club, 287 Goldhawk Road, London W12
Recorded: 13 May 1977
First transmission: 24 May 1977

> Leonard Rossiter . . . . Rigsby
> Richard Beckinsale . . . . Alan
> Frances de la Tour . . . . Ruth
> Don Warrington . . . . Philip
> Roger Brierley . . . . Osborne

Rigsby is fed up to the back teeth with Osborne, a tenant who's a hypochondriac, and to make matters even worse Miss Jones is molly-coddling him by cooking his meals. While all the other lodgers believe Osborne is ill, Rigsby thinks he's taking advantage of everyone, especially Miss Jones.

He confronts Osborne about it, but when the lodger collapses, Rigsby thinks he's dead. He calls an ambulance and breaks the sad news to all the household. Miss Jones reacts to the news by calling Rigsby a murderer, telling him to keep his crocodile tears.

Rigsby wants to make it up to Osborne and give him the best possible send-off. He's mourning his hypochondriac tenant, and begins wondering whether he should have been a little more sympathetic. Down in the basement, Rigsby shows Alan and Philip the coffin he bought in a clearance sale. As it was going cheap he acquired it for himself, but feels it would be best used by Osborne.

Concern over whether the coffin will be too small for Osborne results in Rigsby trying it out for size. Alan and Philip joke around by closing the lid, but can't believe their eyes when Osborne suddenly turns up. When Rigsby finally escapes from the coffin, he thinks he sees a ghost in the shape of Osborne, and passes out.

SERIES 4

1. 'Hello Young Lovers'

Rehearsals: Sulgrave Boys' Club, 287 Goldhawk Road, London W12
Recorded: 17 March 1978
First transmission: 4 April 1978

> Leonard Rossiter . . . . Rigsby
> Frances de la Tour . . . . Ruth
> Don Warrington . . . . Philip

Deborah Watling . . . . Lorna
Alun Lewis . . . . Robin
Robert Dorning. . . . . Father

Love is in the air at the Rigsby household, but the landlord is relieved to find it's not Miss Jones who's in love, although she's very happy for the young couple who've moved in across the landing. Realizing what the young newlyweds mean to Miss Jones, Rigsby scrounges a bottle of champagne from Philip, with which he plans to toast their happiness.

Bearing crisps, flowers and bubbly, Miss Jones, Philip and Rigsby enter the young lovers' room. Assuming it's their wedding night, Rigsby takes a quiet moment to give Robin some advice on love. Miss Jones, meanwhile, finds out from Lorna that they're not married, and her father, who doesn't know about Robin, wants her to finish her degree before settling down.

When Rigsby discovers the truth he storms out, taking the champagne and flowers with him. Later he discusses life's values with Philip and tells him he's asked Miss Jones to contact Lorna's father. But when Miss Jones discovers the man has a filthy temper and collects firearms, she rushes to tell Rigsby, which is just as well because he's mistaken as being Lorna's lover.

2. 'Fire and Brimstone'
Rehearsals: Sulgrave Boys' Club, 287 Goldhawk Road, London W12
Recorded: 10 March 1978
First transmission: 11 April 1978

Leonard Rossiter . . . . Rigsby
Frances de la Tour . . . . Ruth
Don Warrington. . . . . Philip
John Clive . . . . Gwyn

A new lodger arrives: Gwyn Williams, a mature student who's studying theology at the local college. He's a strict, religious man with obscure beliefs and he doesn't like the idea of sharing a room with Philip until Rigsby makes out that he's lost his way and needs someone like Gwyn to guide him. Gwyn relishes the challenge, but on meeting Philip – who's furious he has to share again because he was promised the room to himself – realizes he faces a tough task if he's to steer Philip back on to the straight and narrow.

As it's Wednesday, Rigsby decides to invite Miss Jones downstairs for fish and chips and a glass of white wine, while Philip has a tête-à-tête with Gwyn and convinces him that he's not the one in need of guidance – it's Rigsby – and that Gwyn has been sent on a mission to save him.

After their meal, Rigsby invites Miss Jones to Great Yarmouth, where he'll let her taste the best fish and chips around. When Rigsby nips out to get a cloth after pouring wine all over her, Gwyn bursts in shouting: 'Repent!' He sits on the sofa, holding Miss Jones's hands and discusses the whys and wherefores of going to Great Yarmouth, putting her off the idea.

It's not long before Gwyn has both Rigsby and Miss Jones under his spell, with the landlord singing religious songs, carrying a Bible under his arm, turning off Philip's loud music and ripping up his tabloid newspaper. But when Miss Jones becomes a little too close for comfort, Gwyn decides it's time to move on.

3. 'Great Expectations'
Rehearsals: Sulgrave Boys' Club, 287 Goldhawk Road, London W12
Recorded: 31 March 1978
First transmission: 18 April 1978

> Leonard Rossiter . . . . Rigsby
> Frances de la Tour . . . . Ruth
> Don Warrington . . . . Philip
> Avis Bunnage . . . . Veronica
> Andrew Sachs . . . . Mr Snell
> Gretchen Franklin . . . . Aunt Maud

An official-looking Mr Snell delivers good news for Rigsby: the death of his Uncle George means he's due to inherit fifty grand from the residue of his estate. The thought of such riches puts Rigsby in a joyous mood. The idea of having money to spend goes to his head as he starts booking appointments with his tailor, and he has little time for his tenants, believing they're envious and after his money.

But Rigsby gets a shock when Mr Snell returns to say he forgot to explain about the conditions of the will: he must be married for the money to be released. With Aunt Maud due to come round to check that the condition has been fulfilled, Rigsby thinks no one in the family will remember what his ex-wife looked like, and persuades Miss Jones to take her place with the promise of new carpets.

While Rigsby heads off to pick up his aunt from the railway station, Mrs Rigsby, who's heard about the will, arrives to claim her fair share of the money. The sight of his wife in his house is a shock when Rigsby returns. Even though Aunt Maud declares she'll sanction the release of the money, Rigsby is very unhappy now his wife is back on the scene.

His misery is soon replaced by relief when it transpires no money will be heading his way, because it means he can shunt his wife back to Cleethorpes, where she belongs.

4. 'Pink Carnations'
Rehearsals: Sulgrave Boys' Club, 287 Goldhawk Road, London W12
Recorded: 7 April 1978
First transmission: 25 April 1978

> Leonard Rossiter . . . . Rigsby
> Frances de la Tour . . . . Ruth
> Don Warrington . . . . Philip
> Helen Fraser . . . . Bride
> John Quayle . . . . Groom
> Joan Sanderson . . . . Mother
> Roy Barraclough . . . . Barman
> **Extras:** Colin Martin, Harry Butterworth, Bob Hargreaves,
> Audrey Worth
> **Walk-ons:** Christine Bell, Patrick Lynas, Caroline Tyson,
> Honey Wheeler, Joy Ash, Chris Driver

Desperate for companionship, Rigsby places an advertisement in the personal column of the local rag describing himself as a 'company director in his early 40s who's cultured and sophisticated'. When Miss Jones reads the ad she's keen to meet the man, even though Philip, who knows it's Rigsby's doing, tries to dissuade her.

Rigsby is impressed by the solitary reply, which is covered in scent, so he picks up the phone and arranges a rendezvous at The George, suggesting they both wear pink carnations to identify themselves.

At The George, a peak-capped, dapperly dressed Rigsby tells the barman he's looking for a girl, but when he spots Miss Jones, who tells him she's waiting for a friend, he leaves her alone. What Rigsby doesn't know is that a wedding reception is taking place at the pub, and when he spots an attractive woman sporting a pink carnation he leaps in and lays on what he sees as charm. But when her husband arrives, Rigsby causes total confusion and a row by claiming his wife sent him a letter.

Miss Jones is next to get involved in all the confusion when she suspects the groom is her blind date, and when his wife spots them holding hands, the bride bursts into tears and storms out. Before the escapade is over, Rigsby has accosted the stern-looking mother-in-law and has a laugh with Miss Jones about the whole disastrous affair.

5. 'Under the Influence'
Rehearsals: Sulgrave Boys' Club, 287 Goldhawk Road, London W12
Recorded: 14 April 1978
First transmission: 2 May 1978

Leonard Rossiter	Rigsby
Frances de la Tour	Ruth
Don Warrington	Philip
Peter Jeffrey	Ambrose

Rigsby is having trouble getting the rent from Ambrose, a so-called mystic. They get talking about the lodger's supposed talents, but Rigsby is the greatest cynic. Ambrose says he's most successful with his hypnosis, but can't convince Rigsby to try it out. When Philip enters the room, Rigsby suggests he's a willing patient for Ambrose to test out his skills on. During the experiment Ambrose fails to hypnotize Philip, but accidentally hypnotizes Rigsby instead, taking him back to his childhood, when he caught butterflies and pulled their wings off.

When Ambrose releases him from his hypnotic powers, Rigsby doesn't know anything about it until he finds himself in his long johns. Ambrose's hypnotic powers come in useful again when he helps Rigsby overcome his nerves and tendency to become tongue-tied in the presence of Miss Jones. Rigsby sets about winning her affections with the help of Charles Boyer's accent but ends up with a cream cake pushed in his face.

6. 'Come On In, the Water's Lovely'
Rehearsals: Sulgrave Boys' Club, 287 Goldhawk Road, London W12
Recorded: 21 April 1978
First transmission: 9 May 1978

Leonard Rossiter	Rigsby
Frances de la Tour	Ruth
Don Warrington	Philip
Brian Peck	Ron
Fanny Rowe	Mother

Rigsby's divorce comes through and he's over the moon. He's already got his next matrimonial target in his sights: Miss Jones. She's invited him up for a meal that evening, the ideal time to pop the question and present the diamond engagement ring.

During their candlelit dinner, Miss Jones comments on seeing Mr Rigsby talking to the vicar, so Rigsby grabs the opportunity and says he's been preparing a little speech. Before he can present her with the ring, Miss Jones knocks it on the floor, but Rigsby can't believe his ears when she agrees to marry him.

Miss Jones's mother isn't particularly welcoming when she meets Rigsby, claiming he's old. Even though she had higher hopes for her daughter, Mrs Jones reluctantly welcomes Rigsby into the family after confirming he's insured and his house is freehold.

On the big day, Rigsby's brother, Ron, who's best man, eases the nerves by pouring a drink and suggesting it will be the happiest day of Rigsby's life. But it turns out to be the worst, thanks to his brother taking him to the wrong church and picking a fight with the vicar before arriving at the correct destination three hours too late. But when Miss Jones enters Rigsby's room and admits she stood him up, he is relieved to discover she didn't make it to the ceremony either. He accepts her apologies, playing the sad man, until his brother spills the beans and he ends up with trifle all over his head.

Confetti Casualty

During the closing scenes of 'Come On In, the Water's Lovely', Rigsby grabs a handful of confetti and throws it over Miss Jones and himself. When the scene was being recorded, Leonard inhaled and a piece of confetti got caught inside his nose. As he struggles on, you'll notice him coughing and, when his back is turned to the camera, he tries clearing the offending piece of coloured paper by spitting. Director Vernon Lawrence remembers the situation clearly. 'When he delivers his final few lines, he was in excruciating discomfort; when the scene had finished he went straight to his dressing room and removed the piece of confetti. Fortunately it was the end of the programme; if it hadn't been he couldn't have gone on. But Leonard was a great trouper.'

9

AN EPISODE-BY-EPISODE GUIDE TO EVERY CHARACTER

Eric Chappell's scripts supplied a host of hilarious lines and amusing situations for the central core of characters. But they also introduced a range of additional personnel strong enough in their own right to leave a lasting impression in the minds of the viewers, even though their time on the sitcom was brief. This section explains what every character did in the sitcom. It lists each actor who appeared on the credits of the show, except those discussed more fully elsewhere in the book. If a particular episode is not included, it's because only the main cast members appeared or the performers are described in more detail in another section.

'A Night Out'
The Manager (Frank Gatliff) works as manager of The Grange, an exclusive restaurant where it costs 10p to use the loo. Rigsby, Alan and Philip take Ruth there to celebrate her birthday. Rigsby knows the Manager, Charlie Briggs, but the man's responsibility has gone to his head and he ignores Rigsby. Fed up with Briggs's stuck-up attitude, Rigsby brings him down to earth with a bump by telling everyone his father used to run a tea urn at the market and sold stale sandwiches.

'Charisma'
Maureen (Liz Edmiston) is Alan's girlfriend, who wears shorts and rides a racing bike. Her father doesn't like her dating boys and says he'll wring the neck of the first who touches her. He follows his daughter everywhere, but the bike ensures she can outdistance him. Alan takes

Maureen to his room but she ends up hiding under the bed when Rigsby appears on the scene.

'The Prowler'
Baker (George Sewell) calls himself Detective Constable Baker and suddenly arrives at the house after Miss Jones is frightened by a suspected prowler. Donning the customary detective's mac, he claims he's investigating the incident, even though no one actually rang the police. It turns out he's a criminal, posing as a policeman, and ends up stealing Rigsby's savings.

Policeman (Michael Stainton) is a real policeman who arrives at Rigsby's house during the closing scenes and informs everyone the police are looking for a criminal calling himself Baker.

'Stand Up and Be Counted'
Labour Candidate (Michael Ward) is canvassing in the local elections. Alan and Philip are planning to vote Labour and the candidate pops round to see them at the house.

Mr Platt (Ian Lavender), the Liberal candidate, is new to the political scene. Miss Jones takes a shine to Mr Platt, who drives his mother's mini while out canvassing support, when he comes around to drum up votes.

Mr De Vere-Brown (Anthony Sharp), the Conservative candidate, has Rigsby's support until he turns up, calls him Ragsby and says he'll pull the dilapidated building down if he gets into power. On hearing this vow, Rigsby gives his allegiance to Labour.

'The Permissive Society'
Mr Cooper (George A. Cooper) is the father of Sandra Cooper, whom Alan dates briefly. After his daughter is left in tears, Mr Cooper comes round to the house to establish what Alan's intentions are towards her. When things get nasty, Rigsby steps in and throws Cooper out, only for him to return with his two burly sons.

'Moonlight and Roses'
Desmond (Robin Parkinson) is Miss Jones's bespectacled lover. He works in the local library and hangs around the poetry section looking for poetic quotes he can use to flatter his beloved Ruth. Although a bit

145

of a mummy's boy, he sets his sights on marrying Miss Jones, but their dreams don't work out.

'The Last of the Big Spenders'
Mr Flint (Campbell Singer) is the bailiff who arrives at Rigsby's house to reclaim the furniture because he hasn't paid the bill.
Charlie (Ronnie Brody) is the bailiff's assistant.
The Gasman (Robert Gillespie) takes Rigsby to task when he calls, because Rigsby raided the meter when he needed money to take Brenda out.

'Things That Go Bump in the Night'
Vicar (Norman Bird) is summoned by Rigsby to exorcize the house to rid it of the 'grey lady'.
Curate (David Rowlands) visits Rigsby's house with the Vicar.

'For the Man Who Has Everything'
Fred (Larry Martyn), Rigsby's milkman, finds little festive joy when he delivers on Boxing Day. Rigsby suspects he's having an affair with Mrs Bailey, who lives in the street, because he's seen his milk float outside her house all morning.
Gwen (Helen Fraser) is the postwoman, who's so excited when Rigsby finally receives a Christmas card that she hands it to him personally.
Lucy (Elizabeth Adare) is Philip's girlfriend from Northampton, who visits on Boxing Day. Philip hopes she can rent a room for a few days but confusion leads Rigsby into thinking Philip has brought her along for him.

'That's My Boy'
Mrs Brent (Ann Beach) is offered a room by Alan while Rigsby is sunning himself in Spain. She has a young baby boy, David.
Mr Brent (David Daker) works in the merchant navy, assigned to cross-Channel ferries. Jim returns on leave to see his wife and son.
Radio Announcer (Daphne Oxenford) presents, with great enthusiasm, a children's show on the radio, which Rigsby hopes will entertain Mrs Brent's baby while he is looking after the infant.

'Clunk Click'

Mr French (Derek Francis) is a magistrate whose car Rigsby bumps while he is driving Miss Jones to the country club in his new sports model.

Peppery Man (James Bree), an angry motorist, was to confront Rigsby about his dangerous driving. However, because the recording ran over length the scene was cut, although the actor is still acknowledged in the closing credits and is seen on the back of the recent Granada Media video.

Caroline Armitage (Judy Buxton) is Alan's plummy-voiced girlfriend, who is impressed when she hears he's got a sports car. Her mother is president of the Women's Guild and her father owns most of the property in the area. The only daughter of rich parents, she's worth at least £52,000 in shares and gilt-edged stocks. Caroline is well versed in wine, food and music. She hates bristles and stubble on a man, so Alan finds himself shaving at least twice a day.

'The Good Samaritans'

The Samaritan (John Clive) is called to help the depressed Mr Gray, but ends up coordinating Rigsby's departure on a stretcher.

'Fawcett's Python'

Douglas (Jonathan Elsom), the curate, is a friend of Miss Jones's who rather fancies himself as a singer. He rehearses his rendition of some love lyrics while Ruth plays the recorder. Whenever the curate starts singing, Rigsby has to put Vienna outside because the racket disturbs the cat and she tries getting behind the cooker. Although Douglas has led a sheltered life, he was spotted out on the town with a mysterious woman.

'The Cocktail Hour'

Caroline Armitage (Judy Buxton) – see 'Clunk Click'.

Mrs Armitage (Diana King) is Caroline's mother, who attends a so-called cocktail party thrown by Alan. As expected, Rigsby causes trouble and she storms out, with her daughter following closely behind. The snooty Mrs Armitage is president of the local Women's Guild, but Rigsby sees through her façade, remembering her as Mavis Bagworthy, who used to suffer with a runny nose and go round with her father's rag-and-bone cart.

'Hello Young Lovers'

Father (Robert Dorning) is Lorna's father, who wants his daughter to finish her degree before thinking of settling down. Until Miss Jones phones him, he doesn't know about his daughter's boyfriend, Robin. He is known for his filthy temper and collection of firearms.

'Great Expectations'
Mr Snell (Andrew Sachs) is a bowler-hatted, bespectacled lawyer from Hargreaves Solicitors, who informs Rigsby about his Uncle George's death. Rigsby is in line to receive the residue of his uncle's estate, thought to be in the region of £50,000. Snell later breaks the disappointing news that there's no money left once all debts have been paid.
Veronica (Avis Bunnage) is Rigsby's wife, from whom he's later divorced. When their wedding cake collapsed and his Aunt Maud thought it was a bad omen, Rigsby should have realized his marriage wouldn't work. By the time we first meet Rigsby, the couple have been living apart for some time. Veronica lives in Cleethorpes and seems to have a permanent fag almost falling from the side of her mouth. But when she hears Rigsby could inherit some money, she reappears ready to claim her share.
Aunt Maud (Gretchen Franklin) is one of the executors of the will of Rigsby's Uncle George. She hates Rigsby and always regarded him as shifty.

'Pink Carnations'
Barman (Roy Barraclough) serves the drinks at The George, the pub where Rigsby plans meeting his mystery woman, although she turns out to be none other than Miss Jones.
Bride (Helen Fraser) is the bride who holds her wedding reception at The George. She's sporting a carnation and Rigsby believes she's his blind date.
Groom (John Quayle) is the groom, who gets upset when Rigsby suggests his new wife wrote to him.
Mother (Joan Sanderson) is the bride's mother, who attends the reception at The George.

'Come On In, the Water's Lovely'
Ron Rigsby (Brian Peck) and his brother haven't had anything to do with each other for years, but Ron ends up being Rigsby's best man – until he takes him to the wrong church.
Mother (Fanny Rowe) is Ruth's mother, Mrs Jones, who arrives for her daughter's wedding and doesn't think much of the groom.

10

THE MOVIE

CAST

Rigsby	Leonard Rossiter
Miss Jones	Frances de la Tour
Philip	Don Warrington
John	Christopher Strauli
Seymour	Denholm Elliott
Sandra	Carrie Jones
Cooper	Glynn Edwards
Bert	John Cater
Alec	Derek Griffiths
Italian Waiter	Ronnie Brody
Accordionist	Alan Clare
Rugby Player	Pat Roach
Boutique Assistant	Jonathan Cecil
Workman	Bill Dean

PRODUCTION TEAM

Director	Joe McGrath
Producer	Roy Skeggs
Executive Producer	Brian Lawrence
Screenplay	Eric Chappell
Director of Photography	Frank Watts, BSC
Editor	Peter Weatherley, GBFE
Music composed and arranged by	David Lindup
Musical Supervisor	Philip Martell
Title song: music	Brian Wade
Lyrics	Eric Chappell

Production Manager	Ron Jackson
Art Director	Lewis Logan
Camera Operator	Neil Binney
Assistant Director	Roger Simons
Sound Recordist	Alan Kane
Sound Editor	Terry Poulton
Assistant Art Director	Carolyn Scott
Continuity	Phyllis Townshend
Make-up	Bunty Phillips
Costume Supervisor	Laura Nightingale
Hairdresser	Daphne Volmer
Assistant to Producer	Katy Arnold
Production Accountant	John Bigland
Dubbing Mixer	Bill Rowe
Production Assistant	Jean Clarkson
Choreographer	Janet Jackson
Director of Publicity	Jean Garioch

A Jack Gill Presentation of a Cinema Arts International Production for Black Lion Films. Distributed by ITC Film Distributors Ltd. Certificate: 'A'. Running Time: 96 minutes. Released in 1980. First television transmission: 3 March 1983.

Like most successful sitcoms of the era, *Rising Damp* was transferred to the big screen; but unlike most offerings in this genre, it avoided the pitfalls associated with such a project, mainly by having a script and plot that didn't sag before the closing scene. As a result, the movie was an award-winning product head and shoulders above many of its compatriots. But Eric Chappell, who wrote the screenplay, wasn't enamoured of the end product. 'I wasn't paid a fortune, so didn't feel I had to give it much of my time. The film was basically a regurgitation, with three-quarters of the material coming from the television series; I didn't really do anything new, other than replacing Alan with an art student called John, and introduce a new character, Sandra. But Len carried the film through.'

Not particularly proud of the movie, Eric was shocked when it picked up an award at the Evening Standard Film Awards. 'It was a complete surprise,' he says, because he doesn't think sitcoms convert easily to the big screen. There are enough examples of failed attempts to support Eric's view, but it was well received by many, including a journalist who reviewed the film for *Variety*. He rated it as a 'fairly sharp little comedy', and although he believed it was too parochial to do much business abroad, he felt it would 'pay off prosperously in the home market'. He continued: 'Chappell's screenplay offers a good blend of snappy dialogue to go with some wacky sight gags'. He was equally complimentary about Joe McGrath's directing, regarding it as 'witty and well-paced'.

Roy Skeggs, who produced the film, came up with the idea of adapting *Rising Damp* for the big screen. 'I had experience of such films, having done three, *On the Buses, Love Thy Neighbour* and *Man About the House*. They were all making money, so I started thinking of others we could cover and *Rising Damp* was one,' says Roy, who didn't experience any problems with the film. 'If you're organized and assemble the right team it's like making an extended TV episode. There's a longer schedule and bigger budget but if the performances and direction are good then you have no problems.'

Once Eric had agreed to write the screenplay, Roy had to convince Leonard Rossiter to play Rigsby just one last time, a difficult job bearing in mind that, like Eric, he didn't want to record any more television episodes.

'He wasn't too keen,' says Roy, 'so we took him out to lunch and chatted about it.' While Skeggs wanted an original screenplay, both Eric and Leonard wanted to base the film around storylines from the series. 'I wasn't too keen on the idea, but to keep Leonard's interest I agreed,' Roy explains. 'A script was written and was very good. Leonard had been worried that material no one knew might not help the film, although I think he was being a little difficult for other reasons, money particularly. But the script Eric wrote was acceptable and worked well.'

Joe McGrath, who worked with Leonard on *The Losers*, was hired to direct the film. He met with producer, Roy Skeggs, and he too was keen to avoid simply cobbling together a number of plots already explored in the television series; although he was aware of Leonard's views, he wanted to inject new elements into the screenplay where possible. 'I achieved that by doing a lot of improvisation on the set. Denholm Elliott liked that, whereas Leonard wasn't too happy to begin with, because he was absolutely set in the character and what he'd done before. Leonard started thinking Denholm was only half prepared. He respected Denholm terribly, but after the first few days he took me aside and said he was worried Denholm wasn't word-perfect. I told him that's what happened in a lot of movies, and allowed for improvisation on my part.'

Denholm realized Leonard was concerned he wasn't word-perfect, so started teasing him, as Joe recalls. 'As a joke, although Leonard didn't realize at the time, Denholm asked for his lines to be written on cue cards. The crew, who were in on the joke, wrote a speech for him on a card and stood it against a sauce bottle on the table. When Denholm asked whether everyone was ready to film, Leonard turned to me in shock and said: "Joe, we can't shoot, you can see the card!" It was so funny.'

Running the set was assistant director Roger Simons, who'd worked with Joe on seven previous films. 'You had a nice balance, with Joe introducing fresh ideas and Leonard continuously bringing the ideas and plots back to the character he knew, saying things like: "No, Rigsby would never do that." That's one of the reasons I thought the film worked. And then getting someone like Denholm Elliott, who was a star in his own right, added a different dimension again.'

Joe believes that although Leonard didn't want to pursue the television series any further, he was keen to make a film based on the series, even if he expressed initial reservations. But he was also wary about what lay ahead. 'On television each week he could watch on monitors how the performance was going and more or less control it, but on film there are no monitors to study, so he felt he was delivering himself into the hands of the director; you can do as much as you did in the television series and think you've achieved the performance you want, but through the editing process the director has the power to make or break a character. Leonard felt it was a leap into the unknown as far as playing Rigsby was concerned.'

With no Richard Beckinsale to pick up the role of Alan, another character had to be created, and along came John Harris, an art student. When considering casting, Eric suggested the actor Christopher Strauli, with whom he'd worked on his medical sitcom *Only When I Laugh*. Christopher shared the same agent, Bryan Drew, but when asked to play the character was uncertain whether to accept. 'My first reaction was: "Oh hell!" because Richard was a chum of mine and we'd trained together at RADA. Then I thought: "Well, someone's got to do it, so it might as well be someone who knew him." But I was flattered to be asked.'

The portrayal and development of the character was left to Christopher. 'Therein lay a lot of problems,' he says. 'Leonard Rossiter

The New Tenants

Two new tenants were introduced during the film. In the television episode 'A Perfect Gentleman', Henry McGee played Seymour, but for the movie the veteran film actor DENHOLM ELLIOTT was hired. Elliott, who died in 1992, needs little introduction: during his extensive career he made over sixty film appearances, including *The Sound Barrier*, *The Cruel Sea*, *The Night My Number Came Up*, *Alfie*, *The Night They Raided Minsky's*, *The Rise and Rise of Michael Rimmer*, *A Bridge Too Far*, *Raiders of the Lost Ark*, *The Missionary*, *Trading Places*, *A Room with a View* and *Indiana Jones and the Last Crusade*.

Born in London, Denholm trained at RADA before serving in the RAF during the Second World War and spending three years in a POW camp. He made his stage debut in 1945 and his London debut the following year in *The Guinea Pig*. He went on to become a regular performer in all strands of the profession.

The character introduced to replace Alan from the TV series was John Harris, a mature student studying art. The role was played by CHRISTOPHER STRAULI, who qualified as a teacher in maths and science before joining RADA at the age of twenty-one. His small-screen credits include an episode of *Bergerac*, playing Bunny Manders in *Raffles*, *Romeo and Juliet* and *Measure to Measure* for the BBC, *SOS Titanic* as the chief wireless operator on the *Carpathia*, Toby Lush in the 1987 TV series *Fortunes of War*, *Angels*, *Dempsey and Makepeace* and *Harriet's Back in Town*. But he's probably best remembered as Paul Hatfield in three series of Thames TV's sitcom *Full House*, and Norman Binns in four seasons of *Only When I Laugh*. Although he hasn't appeared on TV for twelve years, he has remained busy working in theatre up and down the country. His West End credits include *The Licentious Fly*, *Lover* and *Season's Greetings*.

wanted me to play it like Richard would have done and made that fairly clear. I told him that, firstly, I was unable to do it and, secondly, I wouldn't want to. Richard had his own unique style and his timing was different from mine. I didn't want to try and do a poor imitation of Richard; I wanted to try and make the character my own.'

Looking back, Christopher admits it was one of the unhappiest experiences of his career. 'It was four or five weeks of unmitigated unhappiness. It was a bad time at home because my wife was having a baby, our second daughter, which was difficult emotionally, and Mr Rossiter was making life pretty miserable at work. But the film turned out fine, and I think I did averagely well, though I could have done better. However, the crew was nice and I found Joe McGrath charming, I liked him immensely.'

Joe sympathizes with Christopher. 'Obviously Don, Leonard and Frances had the advantage of having played their characters for some time and knew them inside out, while Christopher was new to the production. But it's understandable that there was a great sense of loss in Leonard's feelings towards the film since Richard's death.'

Unlike the TV series, which was based entirely in the studio, the budget of approximately £120,000, albeit small in movie terms, afforded producer Roy Skeggs the chance to shoot on location. The principal location required was a property to represent the boarding house, which was eventually found in Notting Hill. Roy thought it important to use a real house. 'I think the subject required it and, in my opinion, worked well.'

Director Joe McGrath was also pleased to use the house, although the filming schedule coincided with the Notting Hill Carnival! 'For a while we considered taking Rigsby out into the street in amongst the crowds but eventually decided against it.' Working with a small cast and production team had its advantages, especially as the film was made during a hot summer. 'The house was small, claustrophobic and very warm. The temperature in some of the rooms was above a hundred and some of us rehearsed stripped to the waist. Normally when you're making a movie there are a lot more people around, but I'm glad this time it was a small team.'

The three-storey terraced house was empty and due for renovation, enabling the film company, renting it for six weeks, to dress it as they liked. 'I wanted to make it look like a slum, so I made it look bleak by repainting walls and hanging awful coloured paper, except for Miss Jones's room, which we made a little prettier.'

Film and television are different mediums and need to be treated as such, but part of the charm of the successful television sitcom was Colin Pigott's excellent sets, depicting all the squalor and dinginess of

Rigsby's boarding house. The compactness of the sets may have thrown up challenges for the production team, but they helped generate a tension which complemented the pace of the show. *Rising Damp* aficionados may argue that the sense of expansiveness generated by using a real property reduced the intensity, pace and friction, some of the sitcom's most appealing features. It may also be argued that the film was perhaps a little more pedestrian and the characters less vivid than what we saw on the box. Joe disagrees with this view. He paid no attention to the look and feel of the small-screen version when it came to directing the movie. 'You need a completely different attitude when using film and there's no way I would have considered making the film using the TV sets. Overall I think it worked well.'

The bigger budget presented opportunities for location filming beyond the house, but fortunately the production team resisted such temptations and kept outdoor filming to a minimum, retaining an affinity with its small-screen cousin. One journalist, writing in a trade magazine, felt it a wise decision not to 'open up too much the one-house setting'. He felt that 'the weakest sequences are the exteriors and the rather foolish dream fantasies.' But he also noted that Joe had 'done a journeymanlike job of making a spin-off look passably like a movie in its own right'.

Although the general plot of the film borrowed heavily from the television series, the screenplay provided the opportunity to inject touches of pathos not seen on the small screen. The agonies and misfortunes of the tenants were examined more closely: Philip is exposed as a fraud when it's discovered he's not the son of an African chief but comes from Croydon, a feature of the original stage play, *The Banana Box*, but not the television series. Miss Jones has a brief affair with Seymour – again something which doesn't happen in the television series, and when she's jilted, Joe spotlights her grief. 'The crew actually applauded at the end of her performance – she's a great actress,' he says. 'Comedy in film really works if you're not trying to be funny. I tried to project the reality of the situation: these are real people in a real house going through real emotions. The characters were trapped in that situation and the actors had to play it for real.'

Other sitcom adaptations have been slated by the press, but *Rising Damp* won great acclaim, as Roy Skeggs explains. 'It was incredible. We had press conferences and executive conferences with viewings afterwards and it went down extremely well. The critics were great and it won awards.' While the movie won the *Evening Standard* award for Best Comedy Film, Rossiter was given the Peter Sellers Award, Denholm Elliott was awarded the Best Actor Award from the *Evening Standard*, Frances de la Tour was Best Actress and Joe McGrath Best Director.

Joe was pleased with the end result. 'I was very happy and felt it worked well. Not having to work in a studio set, which is three-sided, meant we could film from such different angles. I always said that if we'd shot it like the television series all we needed was Leonard standing in two or three different doors and coming in to give the dialogue; we could have shot his scenes first, then turned round and shot the other actors and Leonard needn't have been there. I wanted to get out of the business of Leonard standing at the door giving lines because that was very television. And I feel I achieved that.'

Roy enjoyed making the film so much, he watches it whenever he's depressed. 'I still laugh at it because it's such a funny film. The scene in the restaurant when Rigsby drinks from the finger bowl is hilarious, and it's even better when you know the scene is coming. With most of my films I get bored after seeing them several times, but I never tire of *Rising Damp*.'

11

RISING DAMP ABROAD

An American version of *Rising Damp* was attempted in 1977 but the pilot show was never picked up by a TV station and the idea fizzled out. Initially known as *Joy Street*, but later retitled *Steam Heat*, the pilot was written by Peter Stone and was based on the British episode 'The Prowler'. It was recorded by King-Hitzig Productions of New York for CBS and included Rigsby, Ruth, Alan, Philip, Brenda, Spooner and a cat called Paul Revere, all living at 27 Joy Street. As in the British version, there is also an Inspector Baker, a policeman who arrives to interview everyone about the alleged prowler.

One aspect of the pilot Eric Chappell didn't feel worked well was the portrayal of Philip. 'The actor tried to play the character like Don did but it didn't work out. He played a student, but was almost *too* posh. Don never played it like that and it wasn't what I wanted. It never really stood a chance in America because they had been used to ethnic issues for hundreds of years; I don't think we had anything new to say to the Americans.'

Peter Stone agrees with Eric about the casting. 'The cast was interesting: Jack Weston was the lead and he was fine, but the supporting cast wasn't all that strong – but for all I know perhaps I didn't write it very well!'

Peter was asked to write the script by Alan King and Rupert Hitzig, who produced the pilot for CBS. He recalls: 'It was at a time when British sitcoms were being converted over here and this was another one. It became a failed pilot and, in my view, wasn't good enough. But I saw the British version and liked it.'

Another admirer of the British series was co-producer Rupert Hitzig. 'I thought it was a remarkably good idea for a television show, and we were able to sell the pilot to CBS. We asked Peter, who'd written a show for us before called *Ivan the Terrible*, to write the pilot script and, as far as I remember, we were interested in getting Frances de la Tour to come over and play Ruth; but that wasn't possible, which was a shame because Alan King and I both thought she was wonderful.'

The show was rehearsed for five days and shot in front of a live audience, but the reaction was such that CBS didn't commission a series. 'Pilots are shown to focus groups and if they don't get a 100 per cent positive reaction, the TV station never goes ahead with the show,' explains Rupert. Reflecting on why the programme wasn't given the green light, he feels the setting was partly to blame. 'Our problem was that we don't really have rooming houses like that in the States; the show was funny and got plenty of laughs, but the situation didn't lend itself to the same kind of warmth it received in Britain. So we never went beyond the pilot.'

Given the chance to establish an audience, Rupert is convinced *Steam Heat* would have been successful. 'I think it was wonderful, although I think all the pilots we did were great, but it's hard, sometimes, to fight through the bureaucracy.'

'STEAM HEAT' – PILOT EPISODE

Recorded: Tuesday, 5 April 1977 at CBS Studio 41

Rigsby	Jack Weston
Ruth	Margaret Hall
Alan	Patrick Collins
Philip	Stanley Clay
Brenda	Ellen Parker
Spooner	Jim Fleetwood
Baker	John McMartin
Executive Producer	Alan King
Producer	Rupert Hitzig
Director	Bill Persky
Writer	Peter Stone
Associate Producer	Bob Braithwaite
Art Director	Ron Baldwin

Costume Designer	Domingo Rodriguez
Production Coordinator	Lucy Antek Johnson
Production Assistant	Lynn Finke

Two subsequent attempts to sell *Rising Damp* to the USA followed, both to no avail. In 1985 Buddy Bregman's production company took out an option on the sitcom for two years but failed to attract any interest, while the early 1990s saw Lawson Entertainment, who were successful with *Home to Roost* in the States, do their best to sell the idea, but there were no takers.

While the show never worked for the Americans, perhaps because they tried making their own version instead of going with the original, a Portuguese version has proved very successful. 'It's the first time in Europe anyone has done *Rising Damp*. I can't think why the Portuguese in particular are interested, it obviously said something to them,' suggests writer Eric Chappell.

Eric admits that *Rising Damp* doesn't travel well. 'I've done better with other shows: *Only When I Laugh* and *Home to Roost* have been made in Europe successfully, and the Dutch have done all my shows, except *Rising Damp*. It's strange. But the Swedes are looking at making their own version.'

Although remakes of *Rising Damp* haven't fared too well, the British version shown abroad has proved successful. Eric explains: 'It's been shown on network TV in the States and I've received letters from people over there who've loved the show. It's also done well in Australia.'

12

ERIC CHAPPELL ON SITCOMS TODAY

There is a general feeling today that sitcoms are in decline. I feel that to some extent this is true – although whether it is a decline in popularity or quality is difficult to prove.

The decline began in the late eighties, when TV managements discovered that they could command high ratings by showing second-rate Australian soaps and two-hour, mind-numbing cop shows. Up to this point sitcoms had been the poor bloody infantry of TV – leading the charge, sustaining the most casualties, but gaining the heights.

When I started writing in the early seventies it was quite usual to find that half the top ten programmes were situation comedies. Last week the top sitcom was number twenty-seven.

So has there been a change in public taste? Has sitcom simply become less popular, in the same way that the short story has become less popular in fiction? If it has it's not been helped by the TV planners' lack of faith in the genre. In America sitcoms struck a blip a few years back, but they were persevered with and are now as popular as ever. This has not been so in the UK. My last sitcom, *Haggard*, based on Michael Green's *Haggard's Diary*, was put out at teatime, a children's viewing time, although it was an adult show.

The excuse TV controllers make is that 'we put sitcoms in poor slots because they no longer achieve high figures'. It might just as well be said that sitcoms can't achieve the figures because they are in poor slots. In other words it is a self-fulfilling prophecy.

Another factor which doesn't help is the failure to understand the nature of sitcom. 'Situation comedy' is a terrible title. Comedy is a recurring situation? So what? The comedy should come from the interplay between lively and interesting characters. Where doesn't matter – it's what happens that's important. The idea that we need a comedy for the millennium is to miss the point. All sitcoms inevitably reflect the time in which they are written. *Rising Damp* could only be a child of the seventies; I didn't set out to write 'a comedy for the seventies', it was simply the time I was living in. The reason it's lasted is because we told stories with interesting and original characters – and storytelling doesn't date.

I read somewhere that a certain leading TV executive has declared war on the suburban sitcom, with its lace curtains and three-piece suites. What utter nonsense. Again he's missing the point. Did anyone turn on Shakespeare and say wearily: 'Oh no! Not another palace, Will.' Again it's not where but what that matters.

It is interesting to note that the latest successful sitcoms are in the traditional form. *Dinner Ladies* – a works canteen. *Vicar of Dibley* – a rural vicarage. *Men Behaving Badly* – flatland. *One Foot in the Grave* – suburban retirement. Note that I said 'traditional', not 'old-fashioned'. With stronger language and greater licence they are reflecting the times – they can't help themselves.

But has the public chosen to move away from sitcom? They seem to prefer make-over shows, game shows, cookery programmes, etc. But do they? These programmes are cheap and easy to make, and carry very little risk. Sitcoms are difficult, costly and carry a high risk. So do the public really have a choice? The decline of the sitcom may also have something to do with the decline of the writer's role in TV. The above programmes didn't need a writer and the two-hour cop shows are primarily a director's medium, with long tracking shots and dialogue that could be distilled into fifteen minutes.

Times have changed. Should we, the practitioners, have changed with them? Should we have extended the shows to an hour, dispensed with a live audience, etc? I doubt if that would have helped. To get an hour of comedy drama on TV these days is almost impossible. Have people forgotten how to laugh, or is it that they are not given the chance? Write something with the pure intention of making people laugh and you're already under suspicion. Time and time again the planners seem to prefer turgid melodrama. And it isn't just TV. I've been working in the theatre recently, and what have I found? That light comedy has almost disappeared. But that's another story.

ERIC CHAPPELL, June 2001

13

WHAT A SCENE!

Selecting the funniest scenes from the twenty-eight episodes of *Rising Damp* is almost impossible because Eric Chappell's humour sings out from every page of his scripts. This chapter brings together a few of the choicest moments of life in Rigsby's boarding house.

'The New Tenant' (Pilot)
Alan feels Rigsby doesn't approve of his long hair because he keeps making sarcastic comments, like claiming Alan never attends college because his hair is always wet.

Alan: So that's it, it's my hair isn't it? Now let me tell you, Jesus Christ had long hair.

Rigsby: Now that's enough of that.

Alan: What?

Rigsby: Don't you go comparing yourself with him, you show a bit of respect.

Alan: But it's true. He did have long hair.

Rigsby: But he didn't have a hairdryer did he? Didn't give himself blow waves.

'Black Magic'
With exams on the horizon, Alan and Philip are busy swotting when Rigsby appears on the scene.

Rigsby: You two never stop reading, do you?

Alan: We've got exams.

Rigsby: Ah, we use our brains too much you know.

Alan: No danger of that from you, Rigsby.

Rigsby: Oh I ... nothing wrong with my brain, mate. I passed the scholarship.

Alan:	I didn't know that.
Rigsby:	Ah … never went of course. We were a very poor family. Never stood a chance at the interview – not in gum boots.
Alan:	What's wrong with gum boots?
Rigsby:	Nothing, when it's raining. In the middle of a heatwave they look rather ridiculous. See, very poor, we couldn't afford shoes. Wearing gum boots right through the year branded you, especially round the back of the leg. And children can be very cruel you know. They used to pour water in them; I spent most of the day squirting round the classroom.

'Night Out'

Rigsby talks to Alan and Philip about his limited wardrobe, which contains only his demob suit.

Rigsby:	It's a bit past it now, of course. No, I couldn't wear it, all the lining of the pockets have gone, you know, with carrying too much small change. You put your hands in your pockets, you find yourself clutching your knee caps.
Alan:	Those suits are coming back, you know, they're very fashionable.
Rigsby:	No, no, it's very shiny. If I stand in a strong light I start shimmering.

'Charisma'

Philip teases Alan about his inexperience with girls. Alan responds by reminding him about Maureen, his cycling girlfriend.

Philip:	But you've never made it with anyone.
Alan:	Yes, I have.
Philip:	Alan, I've never seen you with a girl.
Alan:	Well, what about that girl who kept following me?
Philip:	Well, you can't count her, she never dismounts.
Alan:	Ah, she will though, she will, you wait and see.

'All Our Yesterdays'

Rigsby is talking to Spooner and the subject of his broken leg comes up. Rigsby hopes Spooner isn't bearing a grievance because it was Vienna the cat who caused him to fall down the stairs.

Rigsby: You can't blame me and you can't blame Vienna. It's not his fault you didn't see him, I can't put lights on him, can I? I know he feels sorry for you, he likes you, Spooner, that's why he rubbed against your leg.

Spooner: Oh, he rubbed against my legs all right!

Rigsby: I'd have brought him up to see you, only I know his fur gets up your nose. Anyway as long as you don't bear him any ill will.

Spooner: D'you know what I'm going to do, Rigsby, when I get out of this plaster?

Rigsby: No!

Spooner: I'm going to get hold of that flea-ridden monster and wring his scruffy neck.

'The Prowler'

Rigsby feels helping the police brings nothing but trouble and explains a past experience to a policeman.

Rigsby: Listen, listen, I saw a woman knocked down once. It was late at night, she was riding a bike, she didn't have any lights on but it wouldn't have made any difference because the driver was slewed. When I went across she was lying in the gutter. I told the driver what I thought of him, then I went in the box and phoned for the ambulance. While I was in there the rotten sod got in his car and drove off, haven't even got his number.

Policeman: Well, you didn't pass by on the other side.

Rigsby: Just a minute, I haven't finished yet have I. As I was coming out of the box the woman got up, shook herself, jumped on the bike, peddled off down the road – she went like the wind. No one could have caught up with her. When the police and the ambulance came I was the only one there.

Policeman: So what happened?

Rigsby: They arrested me for being drunk and disorderly.

'Stand Up and Be Counted'

During a local election, Miss Jones receives a visit from the Liberal candidate, whom she feels is the most attractive of those in the race.

Mr Platt: Can I depend on your vote, Miss… Miss?

Miss Jones: Miss Jones. Actually, I've always been rather liberal. It's my nature. On the other hand, I suppose I'm what people would call a political virgin – I don't seem able to take the plunge.

Mr Platt: Oh, I see. You mean you're a don't know.

Miss Jones: No, I wouldn't exactly say that. I just need a little convincing.

Mr Platt: Well, of course, the personal approach is most important. That's why I've been going out meeting people, you know shaking hands. We always say you can't beat skin to skin.

Miss Jones: Oh, absolutely.

'The Permissive Society'

Rigsby chats with Alan and Philip and claims Alan has changed considerably since Philip's arrival.

Alan: I haven't changed that much, Rigsby.

Rigsby: Oh yes you have. Before he came here all you knew about women was what you read in those magazines.

Alan: No, it wasn't.

Rigsby: Yes it was! I used to see you hanging around in Smith's, pretending he was looking for 'Practical Woodworker' (*he laughs*). Always turning to the centre pages – he thought all women looked like that you know. It must have come as a great surprise to you to find they haven't got staples across their stomachs.

'Food Glorious Food'

Rigsby has a bet with Philip that he can go without food for forty-eight hours, but he's finding it a trial.

Rigsby: Don't you ever stop?

Alan: You all right, Rigsby?

Rigsby: All right? Do I look all right? I haven't eaten for 36 hours. Hey! Look at my nails, look at those white bits.

Alan: You mustn't worry about that.

Rigsby: It's all right for you, they're not your nails.

Alan: Come on, Rigsby, where's your Dunkirk spirit? Where's your backbone?

Rigsby: If I go on like this you won't have to ask, you'll be able to see it. (*Pointing to Alan's skeleton*). He's in better shape than I am.

'A Body Like Mine'

Before the boxing match, a frightened Rigsby tells Miss Jones what's happening and hopes for a little sympathy.

Rigsby: Miss Jones, I don't quite know how to tell you this, Miss Jones, in fact I really don't know how to tell a woman of your sensitivity and refinement, but there's going to be a fight.

Miss Jones: A fight!

Rigsby: Yes, downstairs, Miss Jones, me and Philip, we're having the gloves on. I'm afraid it's going to be a fight to the finish and the blood's going to flow, so thought it only fair to let you know.

Miss Jones: Oh thank you, Mr Rigsby, I'll come down – I love a good fight.

'Moonlight and Roses'

Rigsby realizes he's got to take action on the Miss Jones front before he loses her to Desmond, but he's not too keen on Alan and Philip's idea of opening his heart.

Alan: When was the last time you took Miss Jones out into the garden and told her exactly what was in your heart?

Rigsby: What … you … you mean I – I – I lov … the three little words?

Philip: He can't even say it.

Rigsby: Well, we don't go for that sort of thing around here, all that moonlight and roses; it's all right for Noel Coward – bet he didn't try it with any of the women round here. You start creeping up on them in a silk dressing gown, you get your fag holder shoved down the back of your throat.

'A Perfect Gentleman'

Rigsby and Alan discuss social class, as Rigsby regards Alan as common.

Alan: I'm not common, what makes you think I'm common?

Rigsby: You eat with your mouth open.

Alan: Everyone eats with their mouth open, Rigsby. What do you expect me to do: stuff it in my ear?

Rigsby: All I'm saying is that once it's in there, that's the last we should see of it. Not with you, though. You're like one of those things on the back of the dustcart, your teeth rotate.

Alan: That's charming that is. How long have you been watching me like this?

Rigsby: It's these little things that give you away in civilised society –
that and smothering everything in tomato sauce. I can just
imagine you at the high table shouting for the sauce bottle
and wiping your butter knife on the tablecloth.

Alan: I wouldn't wipe my butter knife on the tablecloth.

Rigsby: You wouldn't even know which way to pass the port, assuming
you ever let go of it, of course.

'The Last of the Big Spenders'

Rigsby tries borrowing money from Philip because he wants to take out
Brenda, but Philip refuses.

Rigsby: What am I going to do? She's expecting an expensive evening
out?

Philip: You'll have to do what you normally do.

Rigsby: What's that?

Philip: Empty your piggy bank.

Rigsby: Oh, very funny. I can't take her out with a hundredweight of
copper in my pockets, can I? It'll play hell with the linings;
anyway, suppose she sits on my lap, I'll cut her to ribbons.

'Things That Go Bump in the Night'

Alan has returned from taking Brenda to the pictures. Philip is interested to find out how the evening went.

Philip: How did you get on?

Alan: All right.

Philip: Where did you go?

Alan: I took her to see *Doctor Zhivago*; I thought I'd get her in a nice
romantic mood.

Philip: That was good thinking, but did it work?

Alan: She fell in love with Omar Sharif.

Philip: You mean you blew it?

Alan: I didn't blow it.

Philip: Did you kiss her?

Alan: Yeah.

Philip: Where?

Alan: In the balcony.

Philip: I mean whereabouts?

Alan: On the cheek.

Philip:	On the cheek? (*surprised*)
Alan:	Well, she was eating an ice lolly at the time – didn't like the flavour.
Philip:	Well, what happened?
Alan:	There was a big sigh.
Philip:	That could have been a sign of encouragement.
Alan:	No, no, it wasn't Brenda, it was the bloke sat behind me, couldn't see. Dug me in the shoulder blades with his pipe, spent the rest of the night spitting bits of tobacco down my neck.

'For the Man Who Has Everything'

Alan and Brenda arrive back on Boxing Day, thinking Rigsby is at his brother's.

Alan:	Now then, Brenda, alone at last.
Brenda:	What about Rigsby?
Alan:	No, he's spending Christmas with his brother. Can you imagine them two together, setting the dogs on the Salvation Army; pinching pennies off the carol singers. What a Christmas.
Brenda:	Well, what about our Christmas, that wasn't so hot.
Alan:	What do you mean?
Brenda:	I spent most of it rolling balls of wool; your mother doesn't like me, does she?
Alan:	She's just got to get used to you, that's all. You know what mothers are like.
Brenda:	Yeah, I know what your mother's like – she spoils you.
Alan:	I wouldn't say that.
Brenda:	Then why does she blow on your potatoes?

'That's My Boy'

When Rigsby talks to Miss Jones, who's returned to the house, he tells her he went to Spain to get over the disappointment of her departure.

Rigsby:	I tried to lose myself in an excess of gaiety and olive oil, but all I got was boils, and then I thought of you, Miss Jones.
Miss Jones:	Oh surely not, Mr Rigsby, not surrounded by all those flashing-eyed señoritas?
Rigsby:	Ah, they couldn't hold a candle to you, Miss Jones.

Miss Jones: I've never been to Spain, Mr Rigsby. I understand it's very romantic and that the Spanish can be very hot-blooded.

Rigsby: That is very true, Miss Jones.

Miss Jones: Yes, I understand they won't take no for an answer.

Rigsby: Absolutely, I've seen it with my own eyes. No woman is safe there.

Miss Jones: Really, where was this, Mr Rigsby?

'Stage Struck'

Alan and Ruth have been given parts in Hilary's play. While they practise a love scene Rigsby watches.

Alan: Maggie, I'm going to kiss you like you've never been kissed before.

Rigsby: Oh God, this should be interesting (*munching crisps*)

(*Alan pecks Ruth on the lips*)

Rigsby: You call that a kiss?

Alan: And what's wrong with it?

Rigsby: You're supposed to be kissing her, not licking an envelope.

Alan: Well, that does it, I'm not rehearsing with him 'ere.

(*Alan storms out*)

'Clunk Click'

Rigsby thinks he's run over Vienna, but it's only Miss Jones's fox fur. Philip puts the fur in a sack and passes it to Rigsby.

Rigsby: (*Deeply upset*) I'll never drink and drive again. Oh my little boy. There's nothing left of him. Oh he'll never creep up on my lap and stick his claws into my thighs any more.

Philip: Oh never mind, Rigsby. Perhaps he hasn't died in vain, perhaps he's a sacrifice. A warning so that other people might live.

Rigsby: Yes, you may be right. What kills me is that I've just bought thirty tins of cat food for him.

Philip: Oh, never mind, Rigsby, you'll get over it. Would you like to be left alone with your thoughts for a few minutes?

Rigsby: Yes, please, Philip. Thank you very much. You can be very sensitive at times.

'The Good Samaritans'
Rigsby, who believes his new tenant, Mr Gray, is writing farewell letters because he's emigrating, discusses the matter with Alan.

Alan: Why does everyone want to emigrate? I wouldn't go.

Rigsby: They wouldn't have you.

Alan: Course they would with my special skills.

Rigsby: (*Laughing*) Your special … my God; since when has the ability to lie on your back and blow smoke rings been a special skill?

Alan: Look, when I'm qualified I could emigrate anywhere in the world.

Rigsby: Don't you worry, mate, when you start cutting people up, we'll all be emigrating.

'Fawcett's Python'
Rigsby jokes about Alan's reaction upon seeing Marilyn's snake.

Rigsby: You should've seen your face when you came out of the room; talk about blind terror. I haven't seen panic like that since twelve of us tried to get in the same life jacket at Dunkirk.

Alan: It was horrible, it was all coiled and ready to spring. That's what they do you know. They hypnotise their prey and then they swallow it.

Rigsby: It wouldn't have swallowed you, not with those feet. He's really got you going hasn't he – you're really terrified, aren't you?

Alan: No, I'm not.

Rigsby: Yes, you are, you think he's lurking everywhere. You ran away from the garden hose this afternoon.

'The Cocktail Hour'
When Rigsby hears that Alan's new girlfriend, who's coming to visit, has very influential parents, he's excited because he feels it might put his place on the map at long last.

Rigsby: I wish I'd known she was coming, I would have bought that fluffy cover for the toilet seat. Are there any last minute refinements you could possibly suggest?

Miss Jones: Well, Mr Rigsby, you could take those flypapers down and possibly a change of towels in the bathroom.

Rigsby: Good idea, I'll put the blue ones out, they've still got a bit of thread left on them.

'Suddenly at Home'

Rigsby discusses Osborne, the hypochondriac, with Alan.

Rigsby: He's never out of the doctor's. He spends so much time in that surgery they've even consulted him on the new colour scheme.

Alan: You're exaggerating, Rigsby.

Rigsby: No I'm not, he's got his own chair down there. He's only missed once since he was here and that was when he was ill.

'Hello Young Lovers'

While Miss Jones is happy because she's found a new love, Rigsby suffers a pang of jealousy, and launches into a tirade.

Rigsby: Oh, so that's it; who is it this time, Miss Jones?

Miss Jones: What do you mean, Mr Rigsby?

Rigsby: I wondered why you'd been getting out your chocolate digestives. Who is it this time, eh? Who is it this time who's been led on by your cold beauty until he thinks happiness is within his grasp only to find himself discarded like an old sock?

Miss Jones: An old sock!

Rigsby: Until all that is left for him is a quick moment alone with his safety razor – who is it?

Miss Jones: No, no, no, there's no need for all this.

Rigsby: No need! No need! How many hearts are you going to break, Miss Jones?

Miss Jones: I haven't broken any hearts.

Rigsby: Oh yes you have, you break hearts like ... like ... (*he looks around, picks up a handful of biscuits and crushes them into pieces*) this and this and this and this and this ... do you realise what you leave behind, Miss Jones?

Miss Jones: Looks like half a pound of broken biscuits, Mr Rigsby.

'Fire and Brimstone'

Rigsby, dressed in a dinner suit, is enjoying a fish supper with Miss Jones.

Rigsby: Have another glass of wine, Miss Jones. (*He pours the bottle*)

Miss Jones: Do you think I should?

Rigsby: Yes, it'll remove the flavour of the salt and vinegar.

Miss Jones: I must say, that was really delicious.

Rigsby: Yes, yes, you have to know where to go to get a piece of cod like that, Miss Jones. (*Picking his teeth*) It's a very high class establishment. Oh yes, did you notice they always give you those little wooden forks, oh yes, very hygienic. I mean look what happened when they found that glass eye in the batter.

Miss Jones: Glass eye!

Rigsby: Yes, I mean they didn't try to blur the issue by making out it belonged to a killer whale, did they? No, no, they drained the vats and gave everyone their money back.

'Great Expectations'

Rigsby rushes up to Philip's room because he thinks an official from the council has arrived.

Rigsby: I'm trying to avoid someone, I think he's from the council.

Philip: What makes you think that?

Rigsby: Oh, I know the type, he's got those hunched shoulders from crouching over figures all day, and those long, bony fingers you get from squeezing blood from a stone.

'Pink Carnations'

When Ruth tells Philip about replying to the personal ad in the local rag, she admits she once registered with a matrimonial agency.

Miss Jones: They put me in touch with a fun-loving extrovert with an urge to travel. He sounded fine until I found out he was doing five years in Parkhurst. The next one was better, in fact he was quite nice – what there was of him. The trouble was he only came up to my shoulder. The first time I saw him he was sitting on a bar stool – how he got up there I shall never know. We had several Martinis and we talked, oh it was so romantic, until it was time to leave and I had to lift him off the stool.

Philip: Must have been a big disappointment.

Miss Jones: Well, it was, but even then I thought there was a chance, I really tried. I tried so hard I developed a stoop.

'Under the Influence'

Rigsby is talking to Ambrose, one of his lodgers, who claims he's a mystic and can predict the future, something Rigsby ridicules by reminding him of one of his former customers.

Ambrose: I could tell your fortune.

Rigsby: You can't tell fortunes, mate.

Ambrose: I can. I'm the seventh son of a seventh son and we have the gift. We can draw aside the misty veil of time and see the future.

Rigsby: (*Sniggering*) See the fut… you can't see the future. Look what happened when that woman's hair came out and her husband came round; we all knew what he was going to do with that starting handle, you just stood there. Well, he was bound to be distressed wasn't he? He goes to sleep with a flaming redhead and wakes up next to a billiard ball. Listen, mate, if you'd been able to read the future you'd have shinned down the drainpipe.

'Come On In, the Water's Lovely'

While dining with Miss Jones in her room, Rigsby pretends he enjoys a good curry.

Rigsby: I love a good curry, Miss Jones. You can certainly tell it's doing you good by the way the sweat breaks out on your back. D'you know, Miss Jones, I think it's the only thing that keeps those poor devils going in Calcutta, I really do.

Miss Jones: Yes, yes.

Rigsby: You may not know this, Miss Jones. But I happen to be a bit of an expert on Indian food.

Miss Jones: Really, Mr Rigsby?

Rigsby: Yes, yes, oh yes. Tandoori chicken, the Bombay Duck. I particularly like the Vindaloo, yes. Mind you, afterwards it's usually a case of 'where's the loo?' If you'll pardon my vernacular, Miss Jones.

APPENDIX:

RISING DAMP SPIN-OFFS

Over the years, *Rising Damp* has generated the release of videos, audio cassettes, books, a record, and even DVDs. Between 1990 and 1993, Castle Vision issued a series of videos, each containing two episodes of the sitcom, at £5.99 each. *The Best of Rising Damp* featured 'Stage Struck'/ 'Fawcett's Python' (catalogue number CVS5028); 'The Prowler'/'Things That Go Bump in the Night' (EUKV6038); 'Clunk Click'/'Under the Influence' (EUKV6015); 'Food Glorious Food'/'Suddenly at Home' (CVS5030); 'The Permissive Society'/'Moonlight and Roses' (CVS5029). The series was deleted between December 1993 and November 1994. Castle Vision also released six episodes – 'Things That Go Bump in the Night', 'Food Glorious Food', 'Suddenly at Home', 'Permissive Society', 'The Prowler' and 'Moonlight and Roses' – in a two-video pack in September 1991, at £15.79. This was deleted in 1995.

The most recent video releases have come from Granada Media. Three double videos, covering series one (GV0033), series two (GV0133) and series three (GV0165) were released in October 1998, September 1999 and March 2000, respectively, each priced £12.99. Series four (GV0322) was released in March 2001. A *Best of...* compilation, comprising five favourite episodes, has been released by Granada Media.

Two DVDs have been released by Granada Media: *The Very Best of Rising Damp* (GVD008) containing the same five episodes as the video, and the complete first series (GVD020).

Two volumes of audio cassettes, each containing ninety minutes of laughs, were released by the Speaking Book Company in 1992 at £7.99 each. Both were deleted in 1996.

APPENDIX

The film of *Rising Damp*, which was first shown in cinemas in 1980, is still available on video and has appeared in several guises. The most recent was a Carlton product (3007420233), priced £5.99 and released in February 2000. The big-screen version also led to a 45rpm single being issued by Pye on the CHIPS label (CHI 101). The A side was entitled 'Rising Damp' and featured Leonard Rossiter, while the B side, 'Damp Disco', was by The Rigsbyettes.

Two books have been published. Sphere published the first, written by Tony Warren, in 1977. In it Warren, the creator of *Coronation Street*, took highlights from the original episodes and produced a full-length novel (ISBN: 0722189125). It cost just 65p! The second book, by Christine Sparks, was a novelization of the movie, and was released in 1980. Coronet published the book (ISBN: 0340255420) at 95p. The complete scripts of Eric Chappell's *Rising Damp* are due to be published by Granada Media in early 2002.

Finally, the official *Rising Damp* website is currently under construction at **www.comedy-classics.org**. This will provide a feast of information about the show and will be administered by Ian Abraham.

INDEX